To Daryl on his birthday
Mother & Dad

Re : Judge Bell and his *Footnotes to History . . .*

Griffin Bell is one of my personal heroes. In this remarkable book, Judge Bell brings to bear his passion for history and his own rich career in public service to his country to convey with remarkable clarity and insight significant events in our history which helped shape our past and formed a pathway to our future. Those who love our country will love this book.

—William H. Webster, past judge of the U.S. Court of Appeals, director of the FBI, director of Central Intelligence and presently chairman of the Homeland Security Advisory Council

Griffin Bell is an American original, a personality unique in his generation. His legacy as a lawyer, judge, and attorney general of the United States includes his core beliefs in honor, law and country. His exemplary private and public career is acclaimed for independence, courage, and an exceptional legal mind. His personal heroes earn the highest attribute Bell can convey—patriot. This book contains vivid histories about a varied group of principled and very human individuals and their roles in pivotal moments of American history. Each chapter evidences Bell's skill in the sifting and careful evaluation of historical detail and that of an engaging teller of stories, but also how these individuals shaped the values of our national character. Well edited for reading today, this collection of his speeches and papers inspire his and our passion for the future.

—Terry Adamson, executive vice president, National Geographic Society, law clerk, assistant to the attorney general, professional colleague, and friend

In 1986, Walter Isaacson and Evan Thomas wrote a book entitled The Wise Men *that described the role Dean Acheson, Averell Harriman and others had in shaping American foreign policy after World War II. Griffin B. Bell is another American wise man whose impact and influence on the legal profession and a post-Watergate U.S. Department of Justice is enormous.* Footnotes to History *displays Judge Bell's wisdom in full force and also shows his profound understanding*

of American history. Judge Bell is an extremely gifted storyteller. His stories are laced with penetrating insight and refreshingly honest observations. In this collection, he takes on the subject of miscegenation and the debate as to whether Thomas Jefferson fathered children by his slave, Sally Hemmings. In concluding that Hemmings's children were indeed Jefferson's, Judge Bell notes his own experiences in South Georgia where he knew racially mixed black persons who were related to "prominent white families" but then teaches us what this really means with an honest observation that "slavery is always a part of the American story, a thread in our national fabric that cannot be ignored, nor should it be." In another chapter, Judge Bell brilliantly recounts Lee's surrender to Grant with a story that I, as his former law partner, have heard him tell many times over the years. In bringing complex and highly charged legal disputes to a successful conclusion, Judge Bell relates the importance of graciousness and compromise by telling us how Grant allowed Lee's soldiers to keep their horses and mules because "they will need them for spring ploughing". Completely unconditional surrenders do not work in wars, nor do they work in resolving legal disputes. Our nation and the legal profession are fortunate to have this great lawyer's wisdom available to continue to guide us.

—Larry D. Thompson, senior vice president of Government Affairs, general counsel and secretary, PepsiCo, Inc.

Footnotes to History
A Primer on the American Political Character

MERCER
UNIVERSITY PRESS

Endowed by
TOM WATSON BROWN
and
THE WATSON-BROWN FOUNDATION, INC.

Footnotes to History

A Primer on the American Political Character

by
Griffin B. Bell

edited by
John P. Cole

Mercer University Press
Macon, Georgia USA

MUP/H668

© 2008 Mercer University Press
1400 Coleman Avenue
Macon, Georgia 31207
All rights reserved

First Edition.

Books published by Mercer University Press are printed on acid free paper that meets the
requirements of American National Standard for Information Sciences—Permanence of
Paper for Printed Library Materials.

Mercer University Press is a member of Green Press initiative (greenpressinitiative.org),
a nonprofit organization working to help publishers and printers increase their use of
recycled paper and decrease their use of fiber derived from endangered forests. This book
is printed on recycled paper.

Library of Congress Cataloging-in-Publication Data
Bell, Griffin B., 1918-
Footnotes to history : a primer on the American political character / by
Griffin B. Bell ; edited by John P. Cole. -- 1st ed.
p. cm.
Includes bibliographical references and index.
ISBN-13: 978-0-86554-904-3 (hardback : alk. paper)
ISBN-10: 0-86554-904-4 (hardback : alk. paper)
1. National characteristics, American. 2. United States—Poltics and government—
Philosophy. 3. Political culture—United States. 4. United States—History—
Anecdotes. 5. United States—Biography. 6. Statesmen—United States—Biography.
7. Politicians—United States—Biography. 8. Generals—United States—Biography.
I. Cole, John P., 1963- II. Title. E169.1.B433 2008
973—dc22
2008040027

Contents

★ ★ ★

Acknowledgments

This book came to be only because my friends in The Ten were willing to listen to me over the years, and I thank them.

My thanks, as well, to my able assistant, Beth Kroger, who carefully typed these words in various forms.

I also acknowledge the able work of senior editor Edd Rowell at Mercer University Press and his mastery of old sources and new updates.

I also want to thank my wife, the lovely Nancy, who insisted that I put these papers and speeches into book form.

Griffin B. Bell

Editor's Acknowledgments

Judge Bell granted me a rare privilege when he allowed me to share in these stories and to learn from him. I count myself fortunate indeed to have worked with such a find thinker.

We are indebted to Edd Rowell for keeping us on course, and we thank Marc Jolley for his commitment to this project and Jim Burt for his elegant jacket design.

My assistant Carey Wimberly at Macon State College was of invaluable help during the final work on the book, and I thank her for her commitment and good humor.

My thanks go to my father, Jerry E. Cole, for passing on to me his love of country and its history, and to my father-in-law, Charles M. Donovan, for his encouragement and counsel.

Finally, I thank my wife Mary Stewart Donovan and our son Noah. They are very much a part of this work.

John P. Cole

To the Ten

Fellow ruminators of history and thought.

Editor's Note

Griffin B. Bell, Attorney General (1977–1979) under President Jimmy Carter, has spent a lifetime thinking about, talking about, reading about, and writing about American history. More than just an armchair historian, Judge Bell has often done the work of professional historians, poring over materials in libraries and archives, interviewing participants in certain events, synthesizing different strands and themes to arrive at his own conclusions. With his prominence at the bench and bar, Judge Bell also has been from time to time at the center of history himself.

Judge Bell has given thousands of talks and speeches on the law, on the workings of government, on constitutional issues. Some of the material in this book came from such speeches, given before large audiences. However, most of the work in this book was drawn from papers researched and presented to a small, intimate audience known simply as "The Ten."

The Ten traces its origins to 1890s Atlanta, a dinner club devoted to intellectual conversation. Membership is indeed small, drawn often by function of office. For example, the presidents of Emory University and Georgia Tech generally have been represented. Other members come by special invitation, as did Griffin Bell in 1974, when he was on the Fifth Circuit bench.

There are other such clubs in towns and cities across the country, each replicating in its own way the ideal notion of the eighteenth-century coffeehouse. These groups strive for a level of reading and understanding that would make a Benjamin Franklin or John Adams feel at home.

Judge Bell has found in The Ten an outlet for his passion for American history. In recent years, he has added his voice to the chorus of historians and political scientists pointing to the dismal state of Americans' knowledge of their own history. Judge Bell decided to break with tradition and bring some of his papers originally for The Ten, along with some other projects, to public view.

We hope this short volume will serve indeed as a primer on the American political character. In it you will find many footnotes to history, enough nuggets to form your own opinion of what makes the American political system so resilient. Judge Bell suggests that each story from our early history gives a unique trait of the American genius in government. He allows, however, that in this regard, you can and should be the judge.

You will also see why Griffin B. Bell deserves the recognition he continues to receive as a dedicated public servant. This book is yet another gift from Griffin Bell to the American people.

Macon, Georgia   *John P. Cole*

Author's Foreword

The Example of Lewis Franklin Powell, Jr.[1]

I met Lewis Powell shortly after the end of World War II. My wife Mary, now deceased, was a native of Richmond and was a friend of Lewis Powell, and it was through her that I met him. We would visit Richmond from time to time, and a few years later, I had a long trial in Richmond involving a warehouse explosion. In the course of almost two years in preparing for the trial and during the trial itself, I made twenty-nine trips from Atlanta to Richmond, where I saw Lewis Powell quite often. I also knew him from the American Bar Association, where he rose through the ranks to be president.

I saw Justice Powell frequently while I was serving as Attorney General, which was during some of the years while he was on the Supreme Court, and we had dinner together from time to time. He was very interested in the justice system generally and particularly in improving the administration of justice.

Justice Powell also had a great interest in education. He served for many years on the Richmond, Virginia School Board and then on the Virginia State School Board during the years when the Southern region was accommodating its school systems to the *Brown v. Board of Education* and subsequent Supreme Court decisions.

In every sense, Justice Powell was a model of what Virginians think of as a "citizen soldier." In the case of

---

[1] Editor's note. Judge Bell originally presented this account of Justice Lewis Franklin Powell, Jr. (1907–1998) on 7 April 2006 as a lecture before the American College of Trial Lawyers. Justice Powell was an early president of the College, which today sponsors the Lewis Powell Lectures.

Justice Powell, he was not only a citizen soldier but a citizen lawyer and a citizen jurist in the highest tradition of his state.

I knew Justice Powell in another way. Almost immediately after I met him, he found out that I was a native of Americus, Georgia and asked if I had known Harry Bowers, also of Americus. It happened that Harry, a lawyer, and I had been close friends since childhood, and I knew of his death during the War.

Justice Powell began his service in the Army Air Force shortly after the beginning of World War II as an intelligence officer assigned to the 319th Bombardment Group. The Bombardment Group was part of the Northwest Africa Air Forces (NAAF). While visiting Powell's Group in North Africa, Major Harry Bowers invited Captain Powell to transfer to the U.S. Twelfth Air Force, a part of the NAAF, as an intelligence officer under Major General Carl Andrew "Tooey" Spaatz. Powell agreed, and he and Major Bowers served together until Powell was recalled to Washington and assigned to the Special Branch of the Military Intelligence Department, which led to his ULTRA code-breaking assignment. Major Bowers was killed in a plane crash in England, and Powell wrote to Bowers's mother about the crash and to report where he was buried.[2]

This story was told to me by Lewis shortly after I met him in the first year after the war. He had only recently returned from Americus, a long trip by train, to visit with Harry's mother. This tells us much about Lewis Powell, the man.

What of Lewis Powell, the judge? Two Supreme Court cases are informative. Powell's unique experiences as an

---

[2]John Calvin Jeffries, *Justice Lewis Powell, Jr.* (New York: Scribner's, 1994) 71, 73. *ULTRA and the Army Air Forces in World War II*, edited by Lewis F. Powell and Diane T. Putney, USAF Warrior Studies (Washington DC: Office of Air Force History, U.S. Air Force, 1987) 13.

officer and a lawyer equipped him for his role in these cases, and our country is better for them.

The first of these cases, *Snepp v. United States*,[3] presented the issue whether an agent of the CIA is bound by his agreement not to publish a book based on his experiences in the CIA without getting clearance from the CIA. The other is the *Bakke*[4] decision. I had a personal involvement in each of these cases.

Snepp, a former employee of the CIA, breached his agreement not to disclose classified information without authorization and not to publish any information relating to the Agency without prepublication clearance. He published a book about certain CIA activities in Vietnam without submitting his manuscript for prepublication review. The director of the CIA asked the Justice Department to bring a suit against Mr. Snepp for the breach. Mr. Snepp had signed the agreement when he accepted employment with the CIA and again as part of his termination upon leaving the Agency.

Specifically, we in the Justice Department sought a declaration that Snepp had breached the contract and an injunction requiring him to submit future writings for prepublication review, and we also sought an order imposing a constructive trust for the government's benefit on all the profits that Snepp might earn or had already earned from publishing the book. The district court found that Snepp had "willfully, deliberately, and surreptitiously breached his position of trust with the CIA and the termination secrecy agreement by publishing a book without submitting it to prepublication review."[5] The Court also imposed a constructive trust on Snepp's profits.

---

[3] *Snepp v. United States*, 444 U.S. 507 (1980).

[4] *Regents of University of California v. Bakke*, 438 U.S. 265, 317 (1978).

[5] *United States v. Snepp*, 456 F.Supp. 176 (E.D.Va. 1978).

The Court of Appeals for the Fourth Circuit upheld the injunction against future violations of the prepublication obligation.[6] The Court, however, concluded that the record did not support the imposition of a constructive trust on Snepp's profits given the government's concession for the purposes of the particular case that Snepp's books divulged no classified intelligence. The Court concluded that Snepp's fiduciary obligation extended only to preserving the confidentiality of classified material. Judge Hoffmann, a district judge from the Eastern District of Virginia, sitting by designation, dissented from the refusal to find the constructive trust. He wrote that "this was no ordinary contract; it gave life to a fiduciary relationship and invested in Snepp the trust of the CIA." Prepublication was part of Snepp's undertaking to protect confidences associated with his trust.

Snepp filed a petition for certiorari, and the government filed a cross petition. In a most unusual procedure, the Supreme Court granted certiorari on both petitions "in order to correct the judgment from which both parties sought relief." The Supreme Court reinstated the judgment of the District Court in total. This was done in a per curiam opinion which represented the views of six justices, including Justice Powell, and was done summarily, which meant without oral argument. Three justices dissented on the grounds that the constructive trust should not have been imposed since no classified information was divulged. The dissenters read the contractual obligation as being no more than an agreement not to disclose classified information, something which was opposite the view of the majority who read the obligation as depriving the CIA of the right to make its own judgment as to whether what was being published was harmful.

---

[6]*Snepp v. United States*, 595 F.2d 926 (4th Cir. 1979).

The Supreme Court stated that it agreed with the Court of Appeals that the Snepp agreement was "an entirely appropriate" exercise of the CIA director's statutory mandate to "protect intelligence sources and methods from unauthorized disclosure." The Court said that the government had a compelling interest in protecting both the secrecy of information important to national security and the appearance of confidentiality so essential to the effective operation of the foreign intelligence service.

The Court agreed with the lower courts that

> a former intelligence agent's publication of unreviewed material relating to intelligence activities can be detrimental to vital national interest even if the published information is unclassified. The Court went on to say that when a former agent relies on his own judgment about what information is detrimental, he may reveal information that the CIA—with its broader understanding of what may expose classified information and confidential sources—could have identified as harmful. In addition to receiving intelligence on domestically based or controlled sources, the CIA obtains information from the intelligence services of friendly nations and from agents operating in foreign countries. The continued availability of these foreign sources depends on the CIA's ability to guarantee the security of information that might compromise them and even endanger the personal safety of foreign agents.[7]

Did Powell's experience in military intelligence affect his views in *Snepp*? The British distrusted the American security of foreign intelligence and would not allow Americans to participate in ULTRA until May 1943, although they made its product available to American commanders on a careful basis. This distrust was caused in part by a leak from the

---

[7]444 U.S. 507, 511-12.

American Embassy in Cairo by virtue of the Germans deciphering the code used by a military attaché at the Embassy outlining the British operations against the Germans during 1941–1942. The British learned of this breach of security and warned the Americans, who then changed the cipher system in June 1942.

Soon thereafter, *The Chicago Tribune*, the *New York Daily News*, and the *Washington Times-Herald* published stories about the Battle of Midway, disclosing that the U.S. had precise information about the composition of the Japanese Strike Force in the Pacific, thereby tipping the enemy that the U.S. had broken the Japanese code, as it had. The Japanese shortly thereafter changed their code, and the U.S. lost this advantage for a few months until they could break the new code.

Reluctance on the part of the British was a morale factor for the U.S. armed forces, which was partly alleviated when, in 1943, the British relented to the point of training the Powell Group of officers to relay ULTRA information to American commanders.[8]

The Supreme Court in *Snell* pointed out that the Court of Appeals's reversal of the District Court's constructive trust remedy was not proper since trial on remand for punitive damages, as was suggested by the Court of Appeals, would require proof of tortious conduct necessary to sustain an award of punitive damages on retrial, and that might force the government to disclose some of the very confidences that Snepp promised to protect. This trial of a suit before a jury if a defendant so elected, the Court said, might subject the CIA and its officials to probing discovery into the Agency's highly

---

[8]See *ULTRA and the Army Air Forces in WWII*, Powell Interview, 84-85.

confidential affairs, and rarely would the government run this risk. Given such problems in the trial, according to a former CIA Director who testified, the potential damage to national security would preclude such a prosecution.

In the majority's opinion, when the government cannot secure its remedy without unacceptable risk, it has no remedy at all, and the Court went on to hold that a constructive trust with disgorgement of any benefits was the proper remedy. Possibly the reason for the use of the summary disposition in the *Snepp* case is reflected in this language of protecting foreign intelligence sources and methods from the usual litigation strictures.

The per curiam opinion would mirror the views of someone like Justice Powell, who had long experience with foreign intelligence, tracing back almost to the beginning of today's CIA, when General "Wild Bill" Donovan convinced President Franklin Roosevelt that we needed a foreign intelligence capacity of our own if we were to enter into World War II. This was the beginning of the OSS, which later became the CIA. As I have stated, Justice Powell was placed in the Special Branch, a select group in the Military Intelligence Department (a forerunner of NSA) of some thirty officers, using and protecting the methods and secrets of ULTRA.

In organizing the Special Branch, Secretary of War Henry L. Stimson and Assistant Secretary John J. McCloy, both lawyers, decided to assemble lawyers and others who had experience in collecting and analyzing complex factual situations and drawing conclusions from facts. Twenty-eight persons of experience were selected, including lawyers, journalists, an architect, and a geologist, among others.

Powell continued his interest in foreign intelligence through his work with the national security project of the American Bar Association, in which he was one of the founders and a leader.

In his biography of Justice Powell, John Jeffries does not mention the *Snepp* case, but I think it speaks well of the maturity and the practical understanding that is required by our courts in dealing with compelling national interests such as foreign intelligence secrets and the need for the appearance of confidentiality. The majority opinion, considering the implication of First Amendment rights, points out that even in the absence of an agreement, the CIA could have acted to protect substantial government interests by imposing restrictions on employee activity that in other contexts might be protected by the First Amendment.

The role of Justice Powell in the *Snepp* case also demonstrates the wisdom of placing justices on the Supreme Court who have worldly experience that leads to an understanding of the practical workings of the law and the government, whether based on the Constitution or statutes.

The other decision to be considered is *University of California Regents v. Bakke*, an appeal from a judgment of the Supreme Court of California holding unconstitutional a special admissions or quota system for blacks, Chicanos, Asians, and Native Americans to the medical school at UC Davis. The California Court also ordered the admission of Bakke, a white student who brought the suit challenging the special admissions program.

The California Supreme Court applied a strict scrutiny standard to the use of the set-aside admissions program and concluded that it was not the least intrusive means of achieving the goal of satisfying the compelling state interest in integrating the medical profession.

I was Attorney General at the time of the *Bakke* appeal in the U.S. Supreme Court and was a firsthand witness to the great pressures that were visited upon the Justice Department and the Solicitor General's Office seeking to support the set-aside program in an amicus brief. In his biography, Jeffries outlines the pressures in great detail.[9] Many civil rights groups, major universities, and the American Bar Association, among others, were supporting the set-aside plan. The Justice Department, after receiving the views of all concerned, concluded that the set-aside program needed to be reconsidered, but did not favor admitting Bakke until that could be done. In other words, the position was to avoid a final decision.

The Supreme Court made short shrift of this position in its final Order. I use "Order" advisedly since there were several opinions, but no opinion of the Court. The opinion of Justice Powell prevailed upon each point for decision, since he made the fifth vote in two 5-4 rulings.

I was attending a Foreign Intelligence meeting in the Situation Room at the White House when the president called me about 10:30 a.m. to say that the Supreme Court had just decided the *Bakke* case, and he wanted me to hold a press conference at the White House for the White House Press Corps at 1:00 p.m. to explain the decision. I moved with haste to obtain a copy of the decision of the Court. It developed that the several opinions covered 156 pages in the Supreme Court Reports. The opinions, whether for or against the set-aside plan or the admission of Bakke, were controlled by the opinion of Justice Powell, who made the fifth vote on each question.

The Order invalidating the special admissions or "set-aside" program was modified insofar as it prohibited the medical school from taking race into account as a factor in its future admissions decisions. Four of the justices would have reversed the California Supreme Court's decision so as to uphold the set-aside program, and four would have affirmed simply on the ground that Title VI of the Civil Rights Act of 1964 was violated. Justice Powell's opinion, in which four Justices

---

[9]Jeffries, *Justice Lewis F. Powell, Jr.*, 462-63.

joined, restricted Title VI to those racial classifications that would violate the equal protection clause of the 14th Amendment and thus decided the case on constitutional grounds. His position was ingenious and rests on the idea that race can be considered in an admissions policy if it is one among other considerations in assessing whether to admit a particular student. He referred to the Harvard admissions plan as being a proper use of race. It avoided the use of quota or set-asides and was included as an appendix to the Powell opinion.

The great controversy over affirmative action had been reduced generally by the public to the idea that quotas, as the set-aside was termed, were invalid, but goals were permissible. The solution was to use goals which were the least restrictive needed to provide diversity in the student body. It is sufficient to say that Justice Powell alone fashioned a position that is somewhere in between no affirmative action and quotas, thereby finding a practical solution to one of the substantial governmental problems of his time. So our country owes a great debt to a single justice on the Supreme Court who fashioned a way out of the quandary which had become quite divisive. I was able to say at the *Bakke* press conference that "I think the whole country ought to be pleased [with the Powell position and the result]."[10]

In his biography of Powell, Jeffries states that Justice Powell, after his retirement, said that *Bakke* was his most important opinion. I agree. Some proof of this is to be found in the progeny of *Bakke* in the Supreme Court. Two cases involving affirmative action at the University of Michigan were decided in 2003.

---

[10] As quoted in the Jeffries biography, 497.

One, *Grutter v. Bollinger*,[11] upheld a law school admissions program at the Michigan law school. The other, *Gratz v. Bollinger*,[12] invalidated an admissions program giving 20 points out of 100 automatically to minorities.

In her opinion in *Grutter*, Justice O'Connor wrote:

> We last addressed the use of race in public higher education over 25 years ago. In the landmark *Bakke* case, we reviewed a racial set-aside program that reserved 16 out of 100 seats in a medical school class for members of certain minority groups. . . . The decision produced six separate opinions, none of which commanded a majority of the Court. Four Justices would have upheld the program against all attack on the ground that the government can use race to "remedy disadvantages cast on minorities by past racial prejudice." . . . Four other Justices avoided the constitutional question altogether and struck down the program on statutory grounds [and affirmed the admission of Bakke]. . . . Justice Powell provided a fifth vote not only for invalidating the set-aside program [and admitting Bakke], but also for reversing the state court's injunction against any use of race whatsoever. . . .
>
> Since this Court's splintered decision in *Bakke*, Justice Powell's opinion announcing the judgment of the Court has served as the touchstone for constitutional analysis of race-conscious admissions policies. . . .
>
> Justice Powell approved the university's use of race to further only one interest: "the attainment of a diverse student body. . . . " With the important proviso that "constitutional limitations protecting individual rights may not be disregarded," Justice Powell grounded his analysis in the academic freedom that "long has been viewed as a special concern of the First Amendment. . . . Justice Powell emphasized that nothing less than the " 'nation's future depends upon leaders trained through

[11]539 U.S. 306 (2003).
[12]539 U.S. 244 (2003).

wide exposure' to the ideas and mores of students as diverse as this Nation of many peoples."... In seeking the "right to select those students who will contribute the most to the 'robust exchange of ideas,' " a university seeks "to achieve a goal that is of paramount importance in the fulfillment of its mission."... Both "tradition and experience lend support to the view that the contribution of diversity is substantial."...

We do not find it necessary to decide whether Justice Powell's opinion is binding.... More important, for the reasons set out below, today we endorse Justice Powell's view that student body diversity is a compelling state interest that can justify the use of race in university admissions.[13]

The test, then, was whether the admissions policy is sufficiently narrow in scope in meeting the objectives of diversity. The law school admissions plan was approved. The affirmative action plan for the undergraduate school invalidated in *Gratz* also followed the Powell opinion.

And so it happened that an opinion by one Justice became, after twenty-five years, the test used by the *entire* Supreme Court in such cases.

I believe there is some parallel between two Virginians, John Marshall and Lewis Powell. John Marshall was an officer under General Washington during the Revolution. He was wounded during the Battle of Brandywine while serving with Morgan's Raiders. He idolized General Washington and became his leading biographer after our government was formed. He later served as Secretary of State under President Adams and began to first define the role of the Executive in foreign policy and foreign intelligence.[14] As Chief Justice, he

---

[13]*Grutter v. Bollinger,* 539 U.S. 306, 322-25 (2003), from the opinion of the Court delivered by Justice O'Connor.

[14]See, e.g., *United States v. Curtiss-Wright Export Corp.,* 299 U.S. 304 (1936).

wrote decisions that brought an understanding of and a solution to the tensions over power between the Executive and Congress, between Congress and the Supreme Court, between the federal government and the state governments, between the executive and the Supreme Court, and between the federal government and the governed—the people.

What Justice Powell was able to do in constitutional law was to build on these great principles. His approach fits well into what Justice Cardozo told us in his book, *The Nature of the Judicial Process*, that the courts fill the interstices left in statutes by Congress. Justice Powell filled the interstices in the Constitution, as new and developing problems were presented to the Court.

Justice Powell's career as a lawyer and jurist demonstrates a life devoted to citizenship and patriotism and one that reflects great credit on the legal profession and on our country. We can look to earlier "footnotes to history" to see how the American political character has been shaped by the unique personal experiences and qualities of long-ago Americans— soldiers, lawyers, even slaves.

Americus, Georgia *Griffin B. Bell*

Chapter 1

Jefferson the Lawyer
The Notion of Natural Rights[1]

The year was 1757. Peter Jefferson lay dying, but his eye was still towards the future. Peter instructed his wife that their son Thomas, fourteen years old, should receive a "thorough classical education." Peter must have been conscious of his own lack of education, successful though he was. Whatever his intent, Peter's deathbed request led to the education of Virginia's most famous lawyer and one of America's most learned leaders and greatest thinkers.

Peter Jefferson had moved to his own plantation at Shadwell in 1751 after having managed his father-in-law's tobacco lands at Tuckahoe for several years. Peter erected a substantial home and several other buildings at Shadwell, and it is said that he had more than 5,000 acres of land in two tracts, one on the Rivanna River (Shadwell) and another on the Fluvanna River.

Peter Jefferson was a member of Virginia's House of Burgesses and served two sessions in 1754 and 1755. He was also County Lieutenant of Albemarle County.

At his death, Peter had more than sixty slaves, along with horses, cattle, and hogs, according to the inventory of his

---

[1]Editor's note. Judge Bell gave this speech upon receiving the Thomas Jefferson Memorial Foundation Medal for Excellence in Law at the University of Virginia in 1984. The conferring of the medal was preceded by a black-tie dinner at Monticello. That same year, also at the University of Virginia, Aga Khan IV received the Thomas Jefferson Memorial Foundation Medal in Architecture. For this event, the Aga Khan had reserved twenty-five hotel rooms for his large entourage, while Judge and Mrs. Bell reserved only one room.

estate. He was survived by two sons and six daughters as well as his wife.

None of Peter's property was entailed, nor did he follow the law of primogeniture. Shadwell was given to his wife for life. His will provided that Thomas, when he reached twenty-one, was to have either the lands at Shadwell or those on the Fluvanna, as he should choose, along with a share of the live-stock, half of the slaves not otherwise disposed of, and the residue of his estate. The land that he did not choose was to go to his younger brother Randolph, along with a similar portion of the slaves and other property. Until the sons came of age, the property was managed by John Harvey and Peter Randolph, the executors of Peter's will.

In the year 1760, Thomas Jefferson "emerged from the hills," as put by Dumas Malone in his biography of Jefferson,[2] and entered the college of William and Mary in Williamsburg. Malone notes that

> [Jefferson's] future friend and rival John Adams was five years out of Harvard; but Alexander Hamilton, in the British West Indies, was little beyond the toddling stage. George Washington, whose advanced schooling was gained in Indian warfare, had married Martha Custis and was farming at Mount Vernon, hoping that his days of campaigning were over... King George III had ascended the English throne, unaware that in the village which was the capital of the Royal Province of Virginia there was a stripling who would one day denounce him in immortal language.

Jefferson had conferred with his father's executors about going to college. He supposed he would continue his study of

---

[2]Dumas Malone, *Jefferson and His Time*, 6 vols. (Boston: Little, Brown, 1948–1981).

the classics and would learn something of mathematics and would gain a more universal acquaintance in college.

At William and Mary, Jefferson fell under the tutelage of William Small. Jefferson later said that Small probably fixed the "destinies of his life." He had much to do with Jefferson becoming a lawyer.

Small was a Scotsman appointed by the bishop of London to William and Mary's faculty in 1758. There he taught physics, metaphysics, and mathematics. After six years he lost his tenure to a returning faculty member. Small returned to England and never again came to America.[3]

Jefferson's association with William Small for almost three years was the same as having a private tutor. He frequently referred to what he had learned from Small, and it was Small who opened the door of George Wythe's law office to Jefferson. Jefferson studied under Wythe for five years, from 1762 to 1767.[4]

---

[3]Fawn McKay Brodie, another biographer of Jefferson (*Thomas Jefferson, an Intimate History* [New York: Norton, 1974; pbk. repr. with new pagination, New York: Bantam, 1975]), states that Jefferson never saw Dr. Small again. Brodie relates, however, that Jefferson did write to him on 7 May 1775 to deplore the Battle of Lexington. The letter was accompanied by six bottles of Madeira. Jefferson had aged the Madeira in his cellar for eight years. His gesture expressed his gratitude to William Small and demonstrated what would be a lifelong habit of keeping friendships in repair.

[4]Jefferson continued his study of the classics even as he was studying law. Malone says that the family tradition was that Thomas studied fifteen hours of every twenty-four, habitually until long past midnight, only to rise at dawn. He is said to have devoted three-fourths of his time to books. (In a letter to John Adams—10 June 1814—Jefferson wrote "I cannot live without books.") We know also he spent time each day on his violin.

Malone says that, next only to tyranny, Jefferson hated indolence, which he regarded as "the besetting sin of his hospitable Virginia countrymen," and about which he wrote with frequency to his children in later years. He once said that "it is while we are young that the habit of

Some of the Randolph cousins studied law at the Inns of Court in London, but Jefferson would not have been able to afford such training, and thus was fortunate to be taught by George Wythe. In all, Jefferson was at the college of William and Mary for seven years and became well acquainted with Williamsburg's permanent residents. In one sense, Williamsburg became as important for a long period in Jefferson's life as would Shadwell, Monticello, and Charlottesville in later years.

Blackstone's Commentaries had not yet appeared. Wythe started Jefferson on *Coke on Littleton*, which constituted the first of four parts of the *Institutes of the Laws of England.*[5] Jefferson would probably have studied the same book if he had gone to the Inns of Court in London, since it was a lawyer's primer in England for more than a century. The book is said to have brought many eminent men to tears as they tried to understand it, but Jefferson persisted because Wythe convinced him that there was no choice but to conquer Coke. Coke's text was referred to as "crabbed and uncouth," but Jefferson preferred it to what he called the "honeyed words" of Blackstone which he read later and which was much easier for others to understand.

Fawn Brodie describes Wythe as a fine Greek and Latin scholar who was thirty-five years old when he accepted the nineteen-year-old Jefferson as his law student. Wythe was one of the most respected lawyers in Virginia. Brodie says

---

industry is formed. If not then, it never is afterwards." He once said to his daughter, "Determine never to be idle," and that "No person will have occasion to complain of the want of time who never loses any." On another occasion, says Malone, Jefferson observed "[I]t is wonderful how much may be done if we are always doing."

[5]Sir Edward Coke, *The First Part of the Institutes of the Laws of England, or, a Commentary upon Littleton* (orig. 1628).

that in the beginning Jefferson disliked the study of law. He wrote to a friend in 1762: "I do wish the devil had old Coke, for I am sure I never was so tired of an old dull scoundrel in my life."[6]

When Jefferson, in the next decade, moved in the Virginia House of Burgesses that "tenants in fee tail" should hold their lands in "fee simple" and thus acquire a "pure inheritance," he could have reflected that he first learned the meaning of these crucial terms from old Coke himself.

Jefferson was far ahead of his time, however, in what we might today think would be the proper way to study law, that is, to have a classical education before undertaking legal studies. One of his friends wrote and asked him to prescribe a proper reading list for him, although he had already entered the law practice. Jefferson replied that he should employ himself in physical studies, ethics, religion (both natural and sectarian), and natural law. Jefferson added that his friend should read law for four hours a day, four hours on the other subjects, and one hour on politics. He then suggested reading history and studying rhetoric and oratory.

Jefferson was also ahead of his time in studying English cases, outlining or briefing them for the point of law and then keeping a digest of each one. In his practice, he continued keeping a digest, though mainly of cases from England. Only a few reported opinions were generated in Virginia's colonial courts at the time.

Jefferson entered the practice of law in 1767. His law practice was largely before the General Court in Williamsburg. This court's membership included lay persons as well

------

[6]From Jefferson to John Page, Fairfield, 25 December 1762. Wythe was a collector of books, and under his influence Jefferson began collecting also. In fact, according to Brodie, as evidence of his great affection for Jefferson, Wythe bequeathed him his own superb library.

as lawyers and was the court in which equity matters and felonies, among other actions, were tried. In addition, there was a county court in each county, and Jefferson was active in his own county of Albemarle and also in Augusta County, the westernmost county in Virginia.

Jefferson had more than 800 cases during his seven years of practice in the General Court. In addition, he had a busy practice before the Privy Council involving land titles. He was one of the leading scholars in the law, but he was never considered a great trial lawyer. That reputation belonged to Patrick Henry, perhaps the greatest jury lawyer of his time, and other Virginia lawyers. Jefferson's high-pitched voice kept him from speaking loudly to the juries, as was the custom.

Jefferson was highly respected by other lawyers for his scholarly opinion and for his writing ability, but all in all records of his cases would show that his practice was routine, probably boring, and to some extent distasteful. If anything, he may have been overeducated for the law.

Jefferson worked as a lawyer until 1774. By then he had been elected to the House of Burgesses and was enjoying his political career. His diaries show that he was losing interest in law as his interest in political matters gained.

Jefferson's loss of interest in the law and his decision to give up the practice was made possible by the death of his father-in-law, John Wayles, who left a very large estate. Thus, through his wife, Jefferson became a wealthy man and devoted the balance of his life to public affairs, along with the building of Monticello on a little mountain very near Shadwell, gardening, his violin, and, of course, the founding of the University of Virginia.

In August 1774, at the age of thirty-one, Jefferson turned his unfinished General Court practice over to Edmund Randolph. Never again was Jefferson to appear in court.

Edmund Randolph, just admitted to the bar and twenty-one years old, was a kinsman of Jefferson whose father, John, had declined to take Jefferson's practice. Edmund was later attorney general and then governor of Virginia, Washington's army chief of staff, the first attorney general of the United States, and later secretary of state.

While Jefferson left the bar two years before 1776, we still might consider the Declaration of Independence his best legal work. The Declaration is, of course, a political statement, but by its terms it propounds the legal rationale for rebellion. Jefferson in 1776 laid out one of history's best jury arguments.

Many Americans, and many others around the globe, are familiar with the "self-evident truths" of the Declaration of Independence, "that all men are created equal, that they are endowed by their Creator with certain inalienable Rights, that among these are Life, Liberty, and the Pursuit of Happiness." But Jefferson's greatest work does not assume such philosophical statements are sufficient to justify treason. Instead, as any student of Coke and the common law would do, Jefferson lays out his bill of particulars.

Reading the Declaration of Independence in full reveals the Founders' legal basis for their drastic action. Appealing for consent from the jury of English citizens and all nations, Jefferson lists in detail how the British Crown had made the colonists' resistance necessary and reasonable—the common law of self defense.

The Declaration's points, however, are in the style of a closing argument to a jury, not an opening statement. Good lawyers know to restrict opening statements to facts to be proven during the trial. Closing arguments, however, are where lawyers take the evidence and persuade the jury to draw the "right" conclusion. Even appeals to emotion are allowed and proper.

Thus Jefferson pulls out all the stops in his summary of the evidence, condemning the king himself for crimes against his subjects. Jefferson even speaks to the fears and prejudices of his jury, citing Britain's use of "foreign Mercenaries" and "merciless Indian Savages" against the colonists. More importantly, though, Jefferson lists in detail every action taken by George III that no good king would take against English citizens.

The Declaration of Independence is a brilliant jury argument, and some today think Jefferson's prose was meant for public reading.[7] While he may have been no Patrick Henry in the courtroom, Thomas Jefferson proved to be a lawyer without equal in the court of political theory. Perhaps only a student of English law, trained on the colonial frontier, could have made such a case. Peter Jefferson's dying wish for his eldest son was indeed fulfilled.

---

[7]See, e.g., the John Dunlap (printer to the congress) *broadside* of the Declaration, printed in Philadelphia.

Chapter 2

Washington in Defeat
Sacrifice and Perseverance [1]

Historian David McCullough has said that the year 1776 in the American Revolution was one of the darkest times—if not *the* darkest time—in the history of the country:

> The war was a longer, far more arduous, and more painful struggle than later generations would understand or sufficiently appreciate. By the time it ended, it had taken the lives of an estimated 25,000 Americans, or roughly one percent of the population. In percentage of lives lost, it was the most costly war in American history, except for the Civil War.
>
> The year 1776, celebrated as the birth year of the nation and for the signing of the Declaration of Independence, was for those who carried the fight for independence forward a year of all-too-few victories, of sustained suffering, disease, hunger, desertion, cowardice, disillusionment, defeat, terrible discouragement, and fear, as they would never forget, but also of phenomenal courage and bedrock devotion to country, and that, too, they would never forget.
>
> Especially for those who had been with Washington and who knew what a close call it was at the beginning—how often circumstance, storms, contrary winds, the oddities or strengths of individual character had made the difference—the outcome seemed little short of a miracle. [2]

George Washington was placed in command of the Continental Army in 1775. He served until 1783. He was a natural choice, given his prior military service, his post as head of the

---

[1]<u>Editor's note</u>. Judge Bell presented this paper to The Ten on 22 February 2006, George Washington's 274th birthday.
[2]David McCullough, *1776* (New York: Simon & Schuster, 2005) 294.

Virginia militia, and that someone from Virginia, the most populous colony, should be chosen if the Army was to be drawn from soldiers from the thirteen colonies.

The army of which George Washington took command was composed mainly of New Englanders. They were a ragtag lot of soldiers—much on the order of political groups, with officers chosen by election. They had no uniforms and had not been exposed to military training. Out of the group, Washington found two younger officers who became valued generals under him, Nathaniel Greene and Henry Knox.

Washington was unusual in many respects. He had much to lose if the Revolution failed. He was one of the richest men in America, married to the wealthiest widow in Virginia. He was a great horseman, fox hunter, outdoorsman, six feet three inches tall, in good health, and fearless. Time after time he risked death in battle, and no matter the defeats or reversals in fortune, he persevered and appeared imperturbable. He was resplendent in his military uniform and gave every appearance of command.[3]

The event leading up to the Revolution was the occupation of Boston by the British in 1774, and that was followed by skirmishes between the British and the Americans in 1775 at Lexington and Concord in April and then on 17 June 1775 by the Battle of Bunker Hill, where the British suffered heavy losses although prevailing.

The first problem for Washington was the occupation of Boston by the British. Henry Knox, then a twenty-five-year-

---

[3]Washington saw his wife, Martha, in winter quarters over the years of the war but did not return to his beloved Mt. Vernon until the war was over in 1781. In prior years, he had served as an officer in the military, in the Virginia Legislature and the National Congress under the Articles of Confederation. Washington was an Episcopalian who never took communion and chose to pray standing up rather than kneeling.

old major, knew that the French had abandoned a number of artillery pieces at Fort Ticonderoga some 300 miles away. The key ground between the British in Boston and the Americans who had Boston under siege was Dorchester Heights, then unoccupied. Knox came up with the idea of fortifying this high ground with these artillery pieces without the British suspecting that it was being done. He was able to recover the artillery and to put the recovered pieces into position in Dorchester Heights in an overnight maneuver. This forced the British to vacate Boston for Halifax without fighting, which was a great result for the Americans. Washington was a hero. But that was not to be the end of the matter.

Bear in mind that transportation in that time was slow, particularly by sea, given the vagaries of the wind. Washington suspected that the British would next attempt to take New York, and he began moving his army to New York. Just as he suspected, the British began preparing an invasion of New York by assembling a task force in Nova Scotia. This took about three months. Meanwhile, Washington was preparing defenses on New York Island, in Brooklyn Heights, and on Long Island.

The invasion of New York began on 29 June 1776. The total British armada numbered almost 400 ships, large and small, including seventy-three warships, with eight ships mounting fifty guns or more. It was the largest expeditionary force of the eighteenth century, the largest force ever sent forth from Britain or any other nation. It included Hessians for the first time to aid the British. The armada included more than one-half of the armed forces of the British Empire.

The British staging area was Staten Island, and the principal fighting took place on Long Island and then "New York Island" or Manhattan. The Americans first suffered a severe defeat at Brooklyn. Washington was able to retreat under cover of darkness and fog to New York Island with the forces that were left. The Americans then left New York Island for New Jersey, except it was decided to defend Fort Washington north of Harlem to cover the retreat. This led to another disaster with a great loss of men, including three generals being captured.

At Fort Washington alone, the entire garrison of 2,837 Americans surrendered, marched out of the fort between two lines of British and Hessians, and laid down their arms. Washington wept upon hearing the news.

It was about this time (23 December 1776) that Thomas Paine wrote his first Revolutionary War essay with its immortal opening lines:

> These are the times that try men's souls. The summer soldier and the sunshine patriot will, in this crisis, shrink from the service of their country; but he that stands it now deserves the love and thanks of man and woman.[4]

Almost simultaneously with the Battle of Long Island, the Declaration of Independence was adopted by the Congress. This signaled two momentous events. First, the thirteen colonies acted as a country rather than as a federation. Second, rather than continued argument with the British over the on-going disputes, the decision was to become independent of the British.

Given the loss in New York, the Declaration must have appeared almost as a futile act, but it marked a landmark shift in what the Revolution was about.

Washington expected the British to move through New Jersey to take Philadelphia, and he assembled his army,

---

[4]Paine wrote thirteen such essays during the Revolutionary War, later included in a collection entitled *The (American) Crisis* (first published as a collection in 1792). Washington thought this first essay was so inspiring that he ordered it read to his troops at Valley Forge.

decimated as it was after the defeat in New York, on the west bank of the Delaware River to defend Philadelphia. (This was the first crossing of the Delaware River and is not to be confused with the historical event which was to take place shortly on Christmas night and the next morning.) This first crossing took place in early December 1776. Washington advised his staff that he needed to make some showing which would inspire the Americans to keep the struggle going. He decided to recross the Delaware so as to retake Trenton, New Jersey on the morning after Christmas Day. He divided his forces into three parts. It turned out that two groups never made it to Trenton, but the group under Washington did make it and went into battle nevertheless. The trip took all night, and the Americans were two hours behind schedule, but Washington surprised the British and Hessians in Trenton and achieved a great victory.

Washington then headed east and north out of Trenton and attacked the British at Princeton, again with much success. These two battles kept the Revolution alive and emboldened the Americans. Washington decided that henceforth he would fight small battles rather than risk his whole army in major battles.

The Americans lost a battle at Brandywine in September 1777, which opened Philadelphia to the British, and a month later lost another battle with the British in Germantown.

In October 1777, General John Burgoyne surrendered the proud army of British and Hessian soldiers at Saratoga, and this brought the French in as an ally of the Americans in January 1778. The Battle of Monmouth in January 1778 was the last major engagement in the North.

The American Army spent the winter of 1777–1778 at Valley Forge. In the spring of 1778, the British unexpectedly vacated Philadelphia for New York.

Meanwhile, many Americans—later to be well known in American history—had entered the stage. Benedict Arnold had become one of Washington's most respected generals. Lieutenant James Monroe had joined Washington, as had Captain, later Colonel, Alexander Hamilton. General Daniel Morgan was head of the valued infantry sharpshooters. John Marshall, wounded at Brandywine, began his lifelong devotion to Washington and his legacy, becoming one of Washington's leading biographers. A nineteen-year-old Frenchman, Lafayette, also made his entrance and became almost a surrogate son to Washington.

In the interim, England was otherwise occupied in war with France, which began in June 1778, then with Spain beginning in June 1779, and with Holland beginning in January 1781.

This brought the American war to the South. Savannah was captured by the British in 1778, and in February 1779 Charleston was lost. Thus began the Southern campaign in the American Revolution.

In August 1780, the Americans suffered another disaster in the Battle of Camden, South Carolina, but thereafter the fortunes of the South shifted. With the help of the Scotch-Irish settlers in the back country of the Carolinas, the American forces humbled the British and Loyalists at Kings Mountain, Cowpens, and Guilford Courthouse. The British suffered heavy losses in each of these battles. It was said that General Nathaniel Greene's plan seemed to be that even though the British kept winning battles in the Southern campaign, by suffering heavy losses in each battle, there would soon not be much of a British Army left. This proved to be the case.

The Scotch-Irish militia, mainly fighting from home, were easily provoked to fighting the British, their ancient enemy. Their long rifles and guerilla tactics were deadly. One British officer, pointing to the hopeless situation for his country, wrote his father that, in the nature of America, every man was, to a certain degree, a soldier.

This war finally ended at Yorktown with General Cornwallis surrendering his British Army, once it appeared that the French fleet had sealed off Yorktown, preventing Cornwallis from being supplied by sea. Thus ended the fighting, although there was not a treaty signed until 1783 with the Treaty of Paris.

What was the legacy of the Revolution?

First, the British lost the United States. With a modicum of compromise, the states would have assumed their place in the Commonwealth of British nations.

Second, the Revolution gave us George Washington, truly the father of our country. As described in the eulogy written by General "Light Horse Harry" Lee (Henry Lee III, father of Robert E. Lee), Washington was "first in war, first in peace, and first in the hearts of his countrymen."

Washington helped give us nationhood, but of a new kind: a republican form of government rather than a pure democracy; a military subject to civilian control; a presidency relegated to an elected status (Washington himself refusing to be "king" or to serve a third term in office). He gave us an example of government which has been replicated time and again over the course of subsequent history, and gradually will be to the ends of the earth, that we may be a free people, that we may be the authors of our own enterprise, and have peace through strength.

Through his own sacrifice and dogged perseverance, George Washington personified the patriot generation and the patriots' dream. Washington surely questioned the war effort as his poorly equipped, poorly trained, sometimes starving "army" of as little as 2,000 men lost time and again to the world's best fighting force. Whatever his doubts and fears,

Washington kept up the fight long enough to get to know his enemy, to take back the momentum, to give time for the French to join the fray, to give legitimacy to the new American government.

There are lessons here for Americans today. Washington's sacrifice and perseverance are examples to our nation, as the current leading world power. Had Britain sacrificed and persevered half as much as Washington and the Americans, there would be no United States. Even great powers must depend on the resolve of their people to prevail in time of war. "Will" has been as important as "might" in America's history.

In the end, Washington's legacy was America, *e pluribus unum*—out of many, one. We are forever in his debt for his own sacrifice and perseverance.

Chapter 3

Sally Hemings of Monticello

Slavery, Race, and Legacy [1]

Near the middle of his first term as president, Thomas Jefferson came under heavy attack at the hands of James Thomson Callender (1758–1803), a Richmond "investigative journalist." A native of Scotland, Callender was a free-lance reporter who specialized in controversy and scandal.[2] He learned from Jefferson's neighbors that Jefferson had fathered five children by Sally Hemings, a slave at Monticello *and* the half-sister of Jefferson's deceased wife, Martha. In 1802–1803, Callender wrote in detail about this in the *Richmond Recorder* and stated, based upon what neighbors said, that the features of the oldest, Tom, bore a striking resemblance to the president himself.[3]

---

[1]Editor's note. Judge Bell presented the original paper, "Mr. Jefferson and Sally Hemings," to The Ten on 27 January 1994. He made his conclusions, based on the documentary evidence, three years before the publication of Annette Gordon-Reed's compelling *Thomas Jefferson and Sally Hemings: An American Controversy* (Charlottesville: University Press of Virginia, 1997) and four years before the DNA tests on the descendents of Jefferson males and Hemings

[2]How ironic that Callender was a former mouthpiece for Jefferson and the Federalists. It was Callender who broke the story of Alexander Hamilton's extramarital affair in 1796. It was Callender who attacked the Federalists for corruption, who went to jail for those attacks under the Sedition Act (prosecuted by the John Adams administration, tried before Justice Samuel Chase), and who was pardoned by Thomas Jefferson. But President Jefferson ignored Callender's requests for a federal appointment, turning this angry man against him.

[3]As will be seen, there is considerable doubt as to whether there was a child named "Tom" in the group. There were seven children born to

There was also a story about Sally being in Paris with Mr. Jefferson when he was serving as Minister to France.

The Callender exposé led to a great battle between the Federalist press against Jefferson and the Republican press in his favor. Madison and Monroe defended Jefferson, although Jefferson did not defend himself publicly.

Meanwhile, the editors of two newspapers, one in Frederick, Maryland and the other in Lynchburg, Virginia, investigated the Callender stories and concluded that they believed the Callender charges to be well founded.

John Adams, who believed the stories, had seen Sally in London in 1787, while she was *en route* to Paris. She was the body servant to Marie (Polly) Jefferson, age eight. Adams thought it was the natural result of slavery. Abigail Adams thought at the time that Sally was fifteen or sixteen, very handsome, and almost white. She was, in fact, fourteen.

Chief Justice John Marshall, ever the partisan against Jefferson, complimented Callender on his stories. The editor of the *Richmond Examiner* then accused the chief justice of tampering with his own slave women, and thus began the only high-level political scandal in our country over miscegenation.

In the aftermath of these charges, Jefferson was joined at the White House for about two months by his two daughters and two of Martha's young children. Their other children were left at home. This gave some cover to the president and placed a better light on the Sally Hemings problem. The storm blew over, perhaps because of Callender's demise within a few months after his stories were published, and

---

Sally rather than five, but two died in infancy and perhaps the firstborn as well. See below for names and dates of birth of Sally's seven children.

Jefferson went on to be elected in 1804 to a second term as president.

Was there any basis for Callender's charges based on historical facts as they now exist? What personal stories from 200 years ago lie behind the modern DNA tests?

We begin with certain undisputed facts. Mr. Jefferson's wife, Martha Wayles Skelton, died in 1782, when he was thirty-nine years of age, and he promised her on her death bed before several witnesses that he would not remarry. Through her father, John Wayles, Mrs. Jefferson was the half-sister of Sally Hemings, a slave girl at Monticello. John Wayles had three wives, all of whom had died. Jefferson's wife Martha was by Wayles's first wife. Wayles had other daughters by his second wife and none by his third wife. Martha was thirteen when her last stepmother died, and she married at age eighteen. She was the widow of Bathurst Skelton and had a four-year-old son, John ("Jack"), when she married Mr. Jefferson in 1771.[4]

After the death of his third wife, John Wayles had an affair of many years with a slave in his own household. This was Betty Hemings, who was the child of a black slave and an English sea captain named Hemings. Betty had six children born to a slave father when the affair started with John Wayles and had six additional children by him. These children were three-fourths white.[5] One of the six children born to Betty and John Wayles was Sally Hemings, thus making her the half-sister of Jefferson's wife, Martha.

Upon the death of John Wayles in 1773, Betty and the Hemings children came into Jefferson's ownership through

---

[4]Little John Skelton died in 1772, six months after Jefferson and Martha were married.

[5]After Wayles's death, she had two additional children, one by a white man and the other by a black slave.

his wife, and they ended up at Monticello. These basic facts are undisputed. We will next examine the written evidence that presently exists.

A memoir written by one of Sally's children, Madison Hemings, is informative. This memoir is published as an appendix to the book *Thomas Jefferson, an Intimate History* by Fawn M. Brodie, a professor of history at the University of Southern California at the time of the book's publication in 1974. Professor Brodie found the memoir in the records of a newspaper, the *Pike County Ohio Republican*, dated 13 March 1873. Brodie also included as an appendix a memoir by Israel Jefferson, a house servant of Mr. Jefferson, which was published in the same newspaper and which backs up what Madison Hemings had to say.[6]

In the 1870 U.S. Federal Census, three years before Madison's memoir, it was stated that Madison Hemings was a resident of Huntington Township, Ross County, Ohio. He is listed as a mulatto, age 65, born in Virginia, and written on the line containing this information is the following: "This man is the son of Thomas Jefferson!"

Madison's granddaughter, Mrs. Nellie E. Jones of Watseka, Illinois, wrote to the Thomas Jefferson Memorial Foundation, Monticello, on 10 August 1938, stating that she had "a pair of spectacles, silver buckle, and an inkwell that had belonged to Jefferson." She said that her great-grandmother, Sally Hemings, had given them to Madison Hemings, her grandfather. They were then inherited by her mother, Mary A. Hemings, Madison's daughter. Professor Brodie gives this information in a note to the Madison

---

[6]Namely, "Reminiscences of Madison Hemings" and "Reminiscences of Israel Jefferson," appendix 1, parts 1 and 2, pp. 471-76 and 477-82, in Brodie's *Thomas Jefferson, an Intimate History* (1st ed., 1974).

Hemings memoir and adds that "Mrs. Jones was the daughter of Mary A. Hemings, who, according to the Ross County Courthouse records, Chillicothe, Ohio, was married on April 25, 1864, to David Johnson."[7]

Madison Hemings begins his memoir by saying that he "never knew of but one white man who bore the name of Hemings," and that he was an Englishman and his great-grandfather. "He was captain of an English whaling vessel which sailed between England and Williamsburg, Va." His great-grandmother was a full-blooded African, the property of John Wayles. He stated that Captain Hemings was in the port of Williamsburg at the time his grandmother was born and acknowledged that he was her father and had tried to purchase her from Mr. Wayles, who would not part with the child. She was named Elizabeth Hemings.

Captain Hemings resolved to take the child by force or stealth, but his intention reached Wayles's ears and the baby was taken to the great house under Wayles's immediate care. Captain Hemings sailed from Williamsburg shortly thereafter, never to return. Madison said this was the story that came down to him.

Madison went on to say that Elizabeth (Betty) Hemings grew to womanhood in the family of John Wayles and she was taken as his concubine after his wife died. He stated that she had six children by Wayles, three sons and three daughters: Robert, James, Peter, Critty, Thena, and Sally (the youngest). These children went by the name of "Hemings."

Madison then switches to information on Thomas Jefferson as a public figure with additional information on the marriage of Jefferson to Wayles's daughter, Martha. He points out that his grandmother and her children by John

---

[7]Brodie, *Thomas Jefferson, an Intimate History* (1974 1st. ed.) 476.

Wayles "fell to Martha" at his death, along with other slaves, and consequently became the property of Jefferson.

Shortly after his wife's death, Jefferson was elected to the Continental Congress and then in 1784 was appointed Minister to France.

Jefferson took his oldest daughter Martha with him to France, leaving his youngest daughter Maria with relatives to follow him to France. James Hemings, Sally's brother and eight years her senior, also accompanied Mr. Jefferson to Paris. (Madison, not born until 1805, omits the fact that another daughter, Lucy, had been born to Mrs. Jefferson and that this child was also left in Virginia with relatives, but died soon thereafter of whooping cough.) Madison goes on to say that during Mr. Jefferson's stay in Paris, his mother Sally accompanied the youngest child, Maria Jefferson, to Paris as her body servant. He stated that Sally's stay in France was about eighteen months. (In fact, it was twenty-three months.)

Jefferson's journal showed that he had spent unusual sums for finery on Sally and was paying a tutor in French for James and Sally. (Both of Jefferson's daughters were in school at a convent in Paris.) Madison said that his mother resisted returning to the United States with Mr. Jefferson. She and her brother James were just beginning to understand the French language. More importantly, they knew that in France they were free, while if they returned to Virginia, they would be re-enslaved.

Moreover, Madison said his mother had become Mr. Jefferson's "concubine" and was pregnant by him. To get her to return to Virginia, Mr. Jefferson pledged that he would free James and Sally *upon their return*, as well as her children when they reached the age of twenty-one years.

Sally returned with Jefferson to Virginia late in 1789, then gave birth to a child shortly thereafter—of whom Thomas Jefferson was the father—but the child lived only a short time. (As will be seen, this baby may not have died and may have been named Tom.)

Madison went on to say that his mother gave birth to four other children by Jefferson: Beverly, Harriet, Madison, and Eston. (We know also from the records at Monticello that she had two other children who died at or near birth—another Harriet and a child named Edy.)

At this point, it is important to put these seven births in a sequence based on other sources.

1. 1790—child born shortly after Sally's return from Paris; name unknown, unless this was the mysterious "Tom."
2. Harriet—born 1795, died at age two.
3. Edy—born 1796, died in infancy.
4. Beverly—born in 1798.
5. Harriet—born in 1801.
6. Madison—born in 1805.
7. Eston—born 1808 when Jefferson was 65 and Sally was 35.

Madison states that his brother Beverly left Monticello and went to Washington. As a "white" man, he married a white woman and their only child, a daughter, was not known to others to have any black ancestry. He said that Harriet married a white man in good standing in Washington City,

> whose name I could give, but will not, for prudential reasons. She raised a family of children, and so far as I know, they were never suspected of being tainted with African blood. . . . I have not heard from her for ten years, and do not know whether she is dead or alive. She thought it in her interest, on going to Washington, to assume the role of a white woman. . . .[8]

---

[8]"Reminiscences of Madison Hemings," in Brodie, *Thomas Jefferson, an Intimate History*, 473. The records at Monticello as well as statements

Madison stated that his brother Eston married in Virginia and moved from there to Ohio. He lived in Chillicothe several years before moving in 1852 to Wisconsin, where he died shortly thereafter, leaving three children. He was a professional musician, like Mr. Jefferson, a violin player.

As to himself, Madison was named by the wife of James Madison, who happened to be at Monticello when he was born. He remembers his grandmother Betty Hemings on her deathbed in 1808. He points out that he learned to read at Monticello by learning from white children and that Thomas Jefferson, his father, died on the fourth of July, 1826. He describes Jefferson's temperament and kindness and stated that his family was the only set of Jefferson's children by a slave woman. He said Jefferson "was affectionate toward his white grandchildren, of whom he had fourteen, twelve of whom lived" to be adults. Thirteen of these grandchildren were by his daughter Martha, who married Thomas Mann Randolph, and one was by Maria, his youngest daughter, who was married to John Eppes.

Madison describes how strong Jefferson was and how erect he walked up until the time of his death at age eighty-three. Madison was taught the carpenter trade under the charge of his uncle, John Hemings, the youngest son of his grandmother, whose father was also an Englishman. (John was a half-brother to Sally.) Madison stated that he and his

---

of the farm manager would suggest, first, that Beverly and then Harriet, each almost (seven-eighths) white, were allowed to run away by Mr. Jefferson. See also *Jefferson at Monticello*, edited with introduction by James Adam Bear (Charlottesville: University Press of Virginia, 1967) appendix opp. p. 24, following the report by Charles Campbell of his interview, about 1840, of a Monticello slave, "Isaac (Jefferson)," in which Isaac stated that Beverly and Harriet ran away in 1822 and were later freed by Mr. Jefferson.

sister and brothers were taught a trade at age fourteen. They knew that they would be freed at age twenty-one and they were always permitted to be with their mother, Sally. He said that his mother's duties (all of her life that he could remember) up to the time of Jefferson's death, were to take care of Jefferson's chamber and wardrobe, look after her children, and do light work such as sewing. He and Eston were freed at Jefferson's death, although Eston had not yet reached twenty-one. He and Eston rented a house and took Sally, their mother, to live with them until her death in 1835. Parenthetically, Sally died nine years after Mr. Jefferson died. She was 62 years old when she died.

Madison married and moved from Virginia to Ohio with one daughter, Sarah, and had nine children born in Ohio. He recites that two were dead, but those living besides Sarah were Harriet, Mary Ann (this would be the grandmother of Mrs. Jones, who returned the Jefferson items to the Thomas Jefferson Memorial Foundation), Catherine, Jane, William Beverly, James Madison, and Ellen Wayles. (Note the repeated use of family names.) He said that they were all residing in Ross County, Ohio. As to the two deceased children, Madison recites that his son, Thomas Eston, died in the "Andersonville Prison pen" and that daughter Julia died at home.

Upon my inquiry in 2003, the superintendent of the Andersonville National Monument found that Thomas Eston Hemings was not listed as a Union prisoner there. Poor Eston died on 1 January 1865 at the Confederate prison in Meridian, Mississippi. Superintendent Fred Boyles surmises that the Hemings family, like many others in the Union, assumed their lost loved one, known to have died somewhere in Confederate captivity, must have suffered at the infamous Camp Sumter in Andersonville. At any rate, Eston's status as a Union POW who died in captivity lends support to his father Madison's reminiscences.

Israel Jefferson was a waiter at Monticello and also a carriage driver. He gives a good deal of detail in his statement about all of this and how he assumed the name Jefferson at the time he purchased his freedom. He was sold in 1829, after Mr. Jefferson's death, to a Thomas Gilmer, who later became governor of Virginia. Israel purchased his freedom from Gilmer for $500. He married and with his wife moved to Ohio. He recalls Jefferson's death as follows:

> Mr. Jefferson died on the 4th day of July, 1826, when I was upwards of 29 years of age. His death was an affair of great moment and uncertainty to us slaves, for Mr. Jefferson provided for the freedom of 7 servants only: Sally, his chambermaid, who took the name of Hemmings, her four children—Beverly, Harriet, Madison and Eston—John Hemmings, brother to Sally, and Burrell [Burwell] Colburn, an old and faithful body servant. Madison Hemmings is now a resident of Ross county, Ohio, whose history you gave in the Republican of March 13, 1873. All the rest of us were sold from the auctioneer's block, by order of Jefferson Randolph, Jefferson's grandson and administrator. The sale took place in 1829, three years after Mr. Jefferson's death.[9]

(Israel's account is only partially correct. Sally was freed by Jefferson's daughter Martha two years after Jefferson's death in a discreet manner. Beverly and Harriet, it seems, had been allowed to escape several years earlier and are not mentioned in Jefferson's will. By codicil dated 17 March 1826, he did free John Hemings, Joe Fosset, Burwell Colburn, Madison Hemings, and Eston Hemings.)

---

[9]"Reminiscences of Israel Jefferson," in Brodie, *Thomas Jefferson, an Intimate History*, 478. (Note that "Hemings" is here spelled with double-m.)

Israel recalls LaFayette's visit to Monticello and many of the details about life at Monticello. He closes with the following statement about the relationship between Mr. Jefferson and Sally Hemings:

> I know that it was a general statement among the older servants at Monticello, that Mr. Jefferson promised his wife, on her death bed, that he would not again marry. I also know that his servant, Sally Hemings, (mother to my old friend and former companion at Monticello, Madison Hemings,) was employed as his chamber-maid, and that Mr. Jefferson was on the most intimate terms with her; that, in fact, she was his concubine. This I know from my intimacy with both parties, and when Madison Hemings declares that he is a natural son of Thomas Jefferson, the author of the Declaration of Independence, and that his brothers Beverly and Eston and sister Harriet are of the same parentage, I can as conscientiously confirm his statement as any other fact which I believe from circumstances but do not positively know.[10]

Where does this leave us? The principal nineteenth- and twentieth-century biographers of Jefferson denied the truth of the Sally Hemings story, not knowing that "DNA evidence" would come to bear in the future. Dr. Dumas Malone, Jefferson's most prominent biographer, addressed the subject in an appendix to his volume on *Jefferson the President*.

Dr. Malone, who was born in Mississippi and grew up in Cuthbert, Georgia, was an Emory University graduate. Perhaps he could not bring himself to believe the Sally Hemings story. He paid little heed to Madison Hemings's memoir and suggested that Madison could have been the servant who looked life Jefferson.[11]

---

[10]"Reminiscences of Israel Jefferson," in Brodie, *Thomas Jefferson, an Intimate History*, 481-82.

[11]Madison was like Jefferson in one respect; he was a great fiddler,

The trouble with this suggestion is that Madison was not born until 1805. Callender, the journalist writing in 1802, mentioned a boy, ten or twelve years of age, called "Tom" by him, as bearing a sharp resemblance to Jefferson. The age—ten to twelve—would coincide with the birth of Sally's first child just after her return from Paris. The only evidence that that baby died is in the Madison Hemings memoir, written when he was sixty-eight years of age.

James Hemings, Sally's brother, who was in Paris with Mr. Jefferson, was promised his freedom when he returned to the United States and had trained as a chef for Mr. Jefferson. He was freed in 1796 and was given money to get to Philadelphia. Beverly and Harriet escaped at some point, and their escape is noted in the Jefferson records. There is evidence that Harriet was given money to go to Philadelphia. According to a Jefferson letter, James went back to Paris, returned to Monticello, and was planning a trip to Spain. He eventually committed suicide. Thus, there were many ways "Tom" could have left Monticello.

Dr. Malone stated that parentage is hard to prove, but recites the idea that one or the other of the Carr brothers could have been the father, giving as authority Randall, next to be mentioned, and a letter from Jefferson's granddaughter, Mrs. Coolidge, also to be mentioned. The Carr brothers, Peter and Samuel, were the sons of one of Jefferson's sisters, which was said to explain why one or more of Sally's children resembled Jefferson.

Henry S. Randall was another Jefferson biographer. His biography, which was published in 1858, does not contain the Carr brothers defense. Ten years later he outlined the defense,

according to Isaac Jefferson, a former Monticello slave. *Jefferson at Monticello*, 4.

as given to him by Jefferson's grandson on a confidential basis, in a letter to another biographer, James Parton, who published his biography, the *Life of Thomas Jefferson* in 1874. The letter did not come to light until 1951, when it was used in a biography of James Parton.[12] Jefferson's grandson, Thomas Jefferson Randolph, is said to have alleged to Randall that Peter Carr fathered all of Sally's children. Professor Brodie points out that this was virtually a physical impossibility, and even Colonel Randolph seemed to suggest in the same interview that it was not true.

In a letter to her husband dated 24 October 1858, Ellen Randolph Coolidge, Jefferson's granddaughter, states that four children, all almost white, were permitted to run away from Monticello. She said that her oldest brother told her that these children were fathered by Samuel Carr (not Peter.) She does not say that they were Sally's children.

The Randall interview with Colonel Randolph contains Randolph's recollection of his mother on her deathbed in 1836, ten years after Jefferson's death, saying to her sons that the slave who most resembled Mr. Jefferson could not have been Jefferson's child since he and Sally had been distant from each other for fifteen months before the child was born. She asked them to always defend their grandfather. Professor Brodie points to documents and chronologies by other biographers that Jefferson was always near enough to Sally to have been the father of each of her children—in the same

---

[12]See Brodie, *Thomas Jefferson, an Intimate History*, who, on p. 494 (669 in 1975 pbk. ed.), cites the Parton biography: Milton Embrick Flower, *James Parton, the Father of Modern Biography* (Durham NC: Duke University Press, 1951) and, on pp. 494-97, reproduces Randall's letter to Parton. Parton's biography of Jefferson: James Parton, *Life of Thomas Jefferson, Third President of the United States* (Boston: J. R. Osgood, 1874).

house, she says, nine months before the birth of each of the seven children. 1836 happens to be the year that Madison moved from Charlottesville to Ohio—if it is to be implied that he resembled Jefferson, as Dr. Malone thought.

There is evidence that Thomas Jefferson Randolph said at one point in a letter that each of the Hemings children resembled his grandfather.

My own conclusion about the alleged Jefferson-Hemings relationship of thirty-eight years is that Jefferson was the father of the children. We know by observation that such relationships have happened in our country. Miscegenation was frowned upon socially by whites in the South and, perhaps elsewhere, but rarely mentioned in specifics.[13] Many left the South and "passed" as whites during Jefferson's time and later. All of my adult life I have wondered why these descendents, until recent years, never mentioned their white ancestors, at least not publicly.

In perspective, neither Thomas Jefferson nor Sally Hemings was married during their relationship. Sally never had children by anyone else, according to the best evidence. The Jefferson children by Sally Hemings were treated well, but were never recognized by Jefferson or accorded the amenities that flowed naturally to his all-white children or grandchildren. Sally's children were in a state analogous to

---

[13]In my youth in South Georgia, I knew mulattos who were related to prominent white families, although two or three generations removed. I knew a good number of people who had one-eighth or less black ancestry and many could have passed as whites. I was puzzled by the census of 1870 listing Madison Hemings as a mulatto, but I suppose that he could have been a mulatto or done as his brother and sisters Beverly and Harriet had done—pass as white. Much had to do with the color of his wife and thus his children. Perhaps his was a mulatto family. According to his memoir, his wife was only one-half white. Eston was said to "look white."

limbo, never to have the honor or status that legitimate children and grandchildren receive.[14]

One irony is that Jefferson, ever in denial or distress about slavery and his own role in it, gave these children the tools by which they laid the truth bare. Would there ever have been DNA tests on today's Hemingses and Jeffersons had Madison Jefferson not learned to read and write at Monticello? How many family histories, stories of white and black, free and slave, were lost because slaves in general were forbidden to learn those skills? Jefferson, content to let others defend his status by denying the relationship he had with Sally Hemings, unwittingly kept the truth alive by giving his children by her the gift of education.

The greatest tragedy, and triumph, belong to Sally Hemings, always denied her due, but recognized today. Jefferson promised her freedom upon their return from France, but kept her in bondage till after his death. Mother of the children of a founding father and president, Sally was kept a secret because of her own lineage and status. Somehow, though, she nurtured a sense of pride and purpose in her children that has survived in her descendents today.

---

[14]Fictionally, the most apt description of the tragedy of miscegenation and the children is to be found in William Faulkner's book, *Absalom, Absalom*, where there was a controversy between the white and partially white children of the same father with the result of the death of all of the children. In an article in the March 1989 issue of *National Geographic*, Willie Morris, writing about Faulkner and the impact of his writings, told of an English professor at the University of Mississippi who assigned various Faulkner books to students for reports. One black female student told the professor after reading *Absalom, Absalom*, that she was reduced emotionally to the point where she could not make a report. She said that her white grandfather lived in the same Mississippi town as she and always refused to recognize her or even speak to her.

Quite simply, slavery is always a part of the American story, a thread in our national fabric that cannot be ignored, nor should it be. Sally Hemings and her children displayed dignity in the worst of circumstances, and they deserve to be remembered.

Chapter 4

John Marshall the Federalist
American Nationalism [1]

As I think of the contributions of great Americans who were present at the creation of our country—Jefferson, Hamilton, Madison, Franklin, Adams—none, save Washington, ranks higher in my estimation that John Marshall. John Marshall (1755–1835) deserves the enduring gratitude of our nation for his constitutional decisions that helped to mold a strong federal government with a respected judiciary as a coequal branch of government. Marshall wrote more than 500 of the Court's 1,100 decisions during his thirty-five years on the Court (1801–1835), and many were groundbreaking. He dissented only eight times.

Yet there is an aspect of Marshall's views that is perhaps less well known but nonetheless as relevant to current events today as it was to his times. John Marshall believed, both while on the Court and beforehand, in the preeminence of the Executive Branch in the conduct of foreign affairs and the importance of making room for the president to conduct those

---

[1]Editor's note. This chapter is drawn from Judge Bell's lecture "John Marshall: Presidential Power and Foreign Intelligence." In 2008, the John Marshall Foundation awarded Judge Bell the Marshall Medal for Law, and he prepared this lecture for the presentation of the medal. His grandson, Griffin B. Bell III, an Atlanta lawyer, presented the lecture on his behalf. Judge Bell adds: "I wish to acknowledge the able assistance of George S. Branch and Michael C. Russ in the writing of this paper. They have been my partners at King and Spalding for many years, but above all, they have been close and trusted friends. It has been a pleasure collaborating with them in putting to paper my deep admiration for Chief Justice John Marshall."

affairs without excessive interference from Congress or the judiciary.

Marshall reached these views not purely as a matter of legal reasoning and constitutional doctrine. He brought to bear his own practical experience informed by his varied background as a soldier, lawyer, diplomat, state legislator, congressman, and cabinet member. Taken in combination, those experiences led him to believe that a federal system guided by a strong executive arm was essential to preserve a young democracy confronted with external threats from foreign nations and internal tensions from advocates espousing a decentralized form of government.

The context in which Marshall spoke and wrote makes his views all the more noteworthy. When ratified by the states, the Constitution was little more than an untested blueprint for what was then considered by European monarchs to be a radical form of government. There were no models and few precedents to follow. Even the Constitution's authors and advocates like Jefferson, Washington, Hamilton, Madison, and others disagreed, often strongly, about the exact meaning of its provisions and the powers of the different branches of government. The Constitution was a compromise among its proponents and the states' regional interests, and its ratification by the states was hard fought and in doubt until the last moment. Popular and eloquent advocates, like Patrick Henry of Virginia, spoke out against its adoption.

On a broader level, the nation's continued existence was uncertain for many of Marshall's years on the Court. Our finances were in shambles, and we were threatened and mistreated on all sides by major foreign powers that held little respect for our experiment in democracy. In the years following the ratification of the Constitution in 1789 through Marshall's death in 1835 there were multiple threats to our nation's existence from foreign powers. Europe was in flames as the Napoleonic wars raged. Great Britain was the bully of the seas, capable of bombarding and laying waste to our capital and seizing our sailors on the high seas. The British even burned the White House in 1814. One should read Marshall's decisions and understand the views he advanced from this practical, real-world context. He did not think or write in an ivory tower.

Marshall was born in 1755 in a log cabin on what was then the frontier near the town of Warrenton, Virginia, located about fifty miles west of modern-day Washington. He was the oldest of fifteen children. His father, Thomas Marshall, tutored him and was responsible for most of his training. Given the eloquence and scholarship of his written opinions, it is remarkable that John Marshall received only a few years of formal education, studying literature and history with a tutor who was a minister.

Marshall was a patriot and citizen-soldier from the beginning. He enlisted in 1775 at age nineteen with his father in the Culpepper Minutemen to fight the British, and he later joined the Continental Army where he served as an aide to George Washington during the winter of 1777–1778 at Valley Forge. This wartime experience was an early lesson in the need for a strong national union to defend the country, as opposed to a confederation of states pursuing separate regional interests. Over the course of the war, Marshall fought at the battles of Great Bridge, Brandywine, Germantown, Monmouth, Stony Point, and Paulus Hook.

He left the Army in 1781 as a captain to attend lectures on the law at William and Mary College for six weeks and was licensed to practice law that summer. Along with his new wife, Mary Ambler, to whom he remained married for forty-nine years, Marshall began law practice in Richmond with almost no money and, given the brevity of his formal legal training, learned his profession on the job.

His legal talents soon became apparent, and he quickly became a leader of the Virginia bar. He also served in the Virginia legislature during the period of the Articles of Confederation, when he saw firsthand the need for a strong federal government to deal with foreign threats and to overcome the localized, destabilizing regional interests of the states.

In 1788, he served as a delegate to the Virginia convention for the ratification of the Constitution, where he was a leader in the fight for ratification. He faced formidable states' rights opponents and was the floor leader in explaining Article III on the federal judiciary to a hostile Virginia delegation. Virginia ultimately ratified the Constitution by a narrow margin, and Marshall emerged from the process as a respected spokesman for what became known as the "Federalist" position, as opposed to the states rights "Republicanism" of fellow Virginians like Jefferson, Madison, and Monroe.

(As an aside, Marshall and Jefferson, although second cousins on Marshall's mother's side, were political adversaries for most of their careers.)

In 1795, Marshall declined President Washington's offer to become the U.S. Attorney for Virginia. He also declined Washington's invitations to become the U.S. Attorney General in his Cabinet and, later, a minister to France. He told Washington that he needed to focus on building his practice and supporting his growing family.

But in 1797, he accepted President Adams's appointment as one of three ministers, along with Charles Pinckney of South Carolina and Elbridge Gerry of Massachusetts, to negotiate a treaty with France. This led to the so-called "XYZ Affair" where France's foreign minister, Talleyrand (colorfully described by Napoleon as "merde in a silk stocking"), tried unsuccessfully to extort a personal bribe from the three envoys as a precondition to negotiations. Marshall refused to negotiate on this basis, returned to the U.S., and was praised by Republicans and Federalists alike for his actions. His experience in France only reinforced his views about the need for a strong Executive Branch to oversee the nation's dealings with foreign nations.

Soon after his return, he declined President Adams's offer to join the U.S. Supreme Court, suggesting instead that Adams appoint Bushrod Washington, who was President Washington's nephew. But at the urging of Washington and Adams, Marshall did agree to run in 1798 as a Federalist for Congress, representing the Richmond district. He was elected to Congress even though Virginia was the home of prominent Republicans and future Republican presidents like Jefferson, Madison, and Monroe.

On 7 March 1800, while serving as a congressman, Marshall gave a famous speech on the floor of the House concerning his views on the preeminence of the Executive Branch in foreign affairs. At the time, Republicans in Congress were attacking President Adams for having extradited a sailor named Thomas Nash, who had been charged with mutiny and murder aboard a British ship. Adams ordered the extradition under the terms of a treaty, and Marshall defended the president's actions as entirely proper under the Constitution's delegation of authority to the executive to conduct foreign affairs as well as the terms of the treaty itself. Marshall's speech was a masterpiece of advocacy, as even Jefferson acknowledged. In the course of his speech, Marshall stated that

> The president is the sole organ of the nation in its external relations, and its sole representative with foreign nations.[2]

---

[2]Benjamin Munn Ziegler, *The International Law of John Marshall. A Study of First Principles* (Chapel Hill: University of North Carolina Press, 1939; repr.: Clark NJ: Lawbook Exchange, 2005) 323.

It is noteworthy that Marshall spoke out forcefully in Congress in defense of executive power in a hostile political environment. He spoke on behalf of an unpopular president at the end of his term, before a highly partisan and antagonistic Congress. The charge against President Adams was that he had overstepped his prerogative and unlawfully usurped Congress's constitutional powers. Marshall was what we might think of as an Edmund-Burke-style conservative, speaking in the minority, but eventually using his position on the Court to imprint his conservative, nationalistic views in groundbreaking constitutional cases. Marshall took his stand in Congress not for political reasons but because he believed the issue raised a fundamental question of constitutional importance destined to arise repeatedly in the course of the nation's future.

Marshall was correct about this. One hundred and thirty six years later, the U.S. Supreme Court in *U.S. v. Curtiss-Wright Export Corporation*,[3] relied on Marshall's "great speech" to Congress in 1800 as authority for the proposition that the president, not Congress, is the sole constitutional representative of the country in dealing with foreign nations and that the president's constitutional power in the conduct of foreign affairs is greater than in domestic affairs. Like Marshall, the Supreme Court in 1936 stated that this difference in presidential power derives as much from practical reasons as constitutional principles and that it would be unwise for Congress to lay down narrow standards governing the Executive Branch's oversight of foreign affairs.

While that case addressed the narrow factual context of the defendant's sale of arms to Bolivia in violation of a presidential proclamation and joint resolution of Congress, the

---

[3] 299 U.S. 304 (1936).

Court used the occasion to write a lengthy explanation of the fundamental differences between the Executive Branch's powers in foreign affairs as opposed to domestic affairs. In doing so, it also noted that "secrecy in respect of information gathered by [agents of the Executive Branch] may be highly necessary."

When I served as Attorney General for President Carter, I quickly learned the importance of secrecy, speed of action, and the special expertise necessary to conduct foreign intelligence surveillance. For many years, the Supreme Court's opinion in the *Curtiss-Wright* case, which echoed John Marshall's views on the scope of presidential power over foreign affairs, provided the legal foundation for foreign intelligence surveillance practices of the Executive Branch. In January 1977, when I was sworn in as Attorney General, the practice was well established that the Attorney General, as the president's deputy, reviewed applications for electronic surveillance of suspected foreign spies and their collaborators. Foreign intelligence surveillance, including wiretaps, electronic listening devices, and the like, was conducted without a warrant in cases where secrecy and swift action were necessary and the purpose of the surveillance was to gather foreign intelligence. My predecessor as Attorney General, Edward Levi, held the opinion, and I agreed, that some level of judicial involvement in foreign intelligence surveillance was necessary to reassure the public that foreign intelligence surveillance was not being used as a subterfuge to investigate domestic affairs. In the aftermath of the Watergate scandals, Attorney General Levi had sought legislation in Congress to establish judicial procedures for foreign intelligence surveillance, but when I became Attorney General, such legislation was not in place.

Shortly after I was sworn in, I was advised by the Secretary of State that very sensitive, classified State Department information was being leaked to a Vietnamese communist spy. These diplomatic cables and other classified papers were transmitted to Vietnamese government representatives who were in negotiations with our State Department in Paris. The leak of this classified information to the Communist Vietnamese threatened our national security and endangered the lives of American agents. Based on solid information establishing a serious threat to national security, I authorized wiretaps and electronic eavesdropping on a Vietnamese national, Truong Dinh Hung, who had obtained diplomatic cables and other classified papers relevant to negotiations in Paris then ongoing between the Socialist Republic of Vietnam and the United States. Truong used a courier to get the documents to his Vietnamese handlers in Paris. The courier was a very courageous woman, Yung Krall, the wife of an American Naval Officer and a Vietnamese American well connected in the Vietnamese community in Paris. Truong trusted Ms. Krall because her father was Communist Vietnam's ambassador to the Soviet Union. However, unknown to Truong, Ms. Krall was a confidential informant employed by the CIA and the FBI. Through wiretaps and bugs in Truong's apartment, we identified an employee of the U.S. Information Agency as the source of the classified information. With the cooperation of Ms. Krall, the U.S. Attorney's Office in the Eastern District of Virginia prosecuted and convicted the two spies, Truong and his American collaborator, of espionage.

On appeal to the Fourth Circuit, the defendants challenged their convictions on the ground that the surveillance conducted by the FBI without a warrant violated the Fourth Amendment, arguing that all evidence derived from the surveillance should have been excluded.[4] The Fourth Circuit re-

---

[4]*United States v. Truong Dinh Hung*, 629 F.2d 908 (4th Cir. 1980).

jected the defendants' arguments on these points, citing *United States v. Curtiss-Wright*, the decision that had adopted Marshall's doctrine of presidential supremacy in foreign affairs. The Fourth Circuit refused to adopt a rule that would have required the executive to secure a warrant each time it conducts foreign intelligence surveillance. Rather, the court confirmed that evidence obtained by electronic surveillance is admissible in a criminal prosecution so long as the "primary purpose" of the surveillance was to gather foreign intelligence. Interestingly, the Fourth Circuit rested its decision, in part, on the separation of powers. Just as the separation of powers requires the executive to recognize a judicial role when the executive conducts *domestic* security surveillance, so the separation of powers requires the judiciary to acknowledge the principal responsibility of the president for foreign affairs and for *foreign* intelligence surveillance.[5]

While the *Truong* spy case was winding its way through the courts, the Justice Department reactivated its efforts to secure legislation that would establish a secure and quick procedure for judicial review of foreign intelligence surveillance. This effort culminated in the enactment of the Foreign Intelligence Surveillance Act of 1978.[6] One of the sticking points that stalled the legislation during President Ford's administration was a proposed provision whereby the Congress would have acknowledged the doctrine of inherent presidential power in the area of foreign affairs. Immediately following Watergate, Congress was in no mood to make concessions regarding the scope of presidential powers, even in a limited field so clearly mapped out by the Constitution. So

[5] 629 F.2d at 914.
[6] 50 U.S.C. § 1801, et seq.

the section was removed, and President Carter voluntarily agreed to follow the procedures outlined in the statute.

In 1978 and the political and international environment of those times, the procedures set forth in the Foreign Intelligence Surveillance Act provided the flexibility, secrecy, and speed of action that the Executive Branch needed to protect national security against foreign enemies. It also protected the privacy interests of individuals and set safeguards against broad dissemination of private information gathered through electronic surveillance of foreign agents. In my opinion, this statute has served the country well. But neither the statute nor its subsequent amendments should be read as a concession that the president lacks the inherent power to conduct foreign intelligence surveillance absent legislation. Far from it. As John Marshall wisely reminded us, in the field of foreign affairs the president is the "sole organ" authorized by the Constitution to act on behalf of the nation. And judicial authorities, as well as the language of the Constitution itself, support that conclusion.

More recently, in a case arising out of the bombing of the U.S. embassies in Kenya and Tanzania, the district court in New York ruled that the president has the power to authorize electronic surveillance of American citizens abroad when they are acting as agents of foreign powers, such as the Bin Laden terrorist organization, Al-Qaeda.[7] Following the 11 September 2001 attack and the 2001 Patriot Act, the statutory Court of Review considered the first appeal from an order of the Foreign Intelligence Surveillance Court.[8] The Review Court, comprised of three Senior Circuit Judges, held that the president has the power to conduct electronic surveillance

---

[7]*United States v. Bin Laden*, 126 F. Supp. 2d 264 (S.D.N.Y. 2000).
[8]*In re Sealed Case*, 310 F.3d 717 (Review Court 2002).

without a warrant when "a significant purpose" of the electronic surveillance is to acquire foreign intelligence information even though the information may serve a criminal prosecution purpose as well. The Review Court determined that the "primary purpose" requirement of *Truong* was too narrow and that its limitation on the use of information obtained through foreign intelligence surveillance had led to artificial barriers that impaired sharing intelligence among our counterespionage agencies. Thus, judicial authority has now moved closer to Marshall's view of the preeminence of the president's powers in the field of foreign affairs, particularly where foreign intelligence is concerned.

To be meaningful, the president's power over foreign affairs must include the authority to gather foreign intelligence necessary to protect the nation's secrets against penetration by foreign agents and their collaborators. Legislation that does not interfere with the exercise of the president's power over foreign intelligence surveillance while providing protection of an individual's privacy interests serves a useful purpose. Legislation that goes too far and interferes with the president's prerogatives to gather foreign intelligence violates the Constitution and the separation of powers.

During the Marshall Court's years the nation faced enormous challenges and threats from external forces trying to subvert a young democracy and impose their will on a weaker nation. Like today, the assertion that the Executive Branch aspires to be preeminent in overseeing national security and foreign affairs was an unpopular position in Marshall's day, attacked by many in Congress as undemocratic. Popular presidents like Jefferson, Madison, Monroe, and Jackson, while respecting Marshall's legal talents, attacked his views that conflicted with their brand of republicanism. They sometimes openly challenged the Supreme Court and disregarded its rulings.

Griffin B. Bell

Faced with those attacks, Marshall brought to bear not only towering legal skills but also common sense and shrewdness in recognizing the need for a strong executive to protect and defend the country. In those days, the threats originated with different foreign enemies, but they are no less real today. We now have more intrusive and rapid methods of surveillance and communication such as wiretapping, instantaneous electronic communications, wire transfers of money, the internet, and other facilities of modern technology. Marshall could not have foreseen those sophisticated methods of surveillance and other developments, any more than he could have foreseen the means and destructive power of terrorist acts such as we saw at the World Trade Center on "9/11." But he had the foresight to understand that the country must have a strong executive arm to safeguard the nation's security against foreign enemies.

Not all our founding fathers shared Marshall's vision. Thomas Jefferson, for example, sharply disputed Marshall's view of the powers delegated to the federal government by the Constitution, particularly where state interests conflicted with federal domestic policy.

Jefferson believed in state supremacy. As the secret author of the resolutions adopted by the Kentucky legislature in November 1799 declaring "void and of no force" the Alien and Sedition Acts, Jefferson advanced the theory of state nullification. Some believe that if Jefferson had served with Washington and Marshall at Valley Forge he might have seen more clearly the merit in the Federalist position, as well as the dangers lurking in the doctrine he espoused. The legacy of Jefferson's state nullification theory was our Civil War, which followed only sixty-two years later.

John Marshall, on the other hand, saw our constitutional union as more than Jefferson's vision of a confederation of sovereign states. In Marshall's view, the people themselves, not the states, had created and approved our Constitution. As a consequence, the Union owed its existence directly to the people, and the federal government was the ultimate sovereign under this constitutional scheme.

On one salient point, however, Jefferson and Marshall were of one mind. In the field of foreign affairs Jefferson did not shrink from using the exclusive powers granted to the president by the Constitution in dealing with foreign powers. By deeds, if not words, Jefferson embraced Marshall's doctrine that "[t]he president is the sole organ of the nation in its external relations, and its sole representative with foreign nations."

Despite criticisms from Marshall's contemporaries, history has proven Marshall's view of presidential power over foreign relations to be valid and essential to the security of the nation.

Justice Oliver Wendell Holmes, on the occasion of the one hundredth anniversary of the day on which Marshall took his seat as chief justice, remembered Marshall's legacy:

> [T]here fell to Marshall perhaps the greatest place that ever was filled by a judge; but when I consider his might, his justice, and his wisdom, I do fully believe that if American law were to be represented by a single figure, skeptic and worshipper alike would agree without dispute that the figure could be but one alone, and that one John Marshall.[9]

---

[9]*The Essential Holmes: Selections from the Letters, Speeches, Judicial Opinions, and Other Writings of Oliver Wendell Holmes, Jr.*, ed. and with an intro. by Richard A. Posner (Chicago: University of Chicago Press, 1992, 1996) 208.

Chapter 5

Jefferson and His Religion
Separation of Church and State [1]

Introductory Note

My interest in Thomas Jefferson was heightened because I had the privilege of knowing his great biographer, Dr. Dumas Malone. Dr. Malone spent over forty years, while teaching at Yale and at the University of Virginia, in writing the biography. Upon his death, he was referred to as the "Sage of Jefferson" in a full-page article in the *New York Times*.

I had occasion to meet Dr. Malone in the early 1980s while he was still teaching in the political science department at the University of Virginia. One of the wonderful experiences that I had at the Thomas Jefferson award dinner was to have lunch at the Miller Center with the senior political scientists on the University of Virginia faculty. I was seated next to Dr. Malone.

Dr. Malone grew up in Cuthbert, Georgia, where his father was president of Andrew College. He received his undergraduate education at Emory University and had not been to Cuthbert since 1921. I urged him to visit Cuthbert and offered to arrange for air transportation, but he declined on the grounds that he did not believe that airplanes could get into Cuthbert.

I now look at Thomas Jefferson's approach to religion and have relied largely on Dr. Malone's biography for this.[2]

---

[1]<u>Editor's note</u>. These observations of Thomas Jefferson's religious views are drawn from a paper Judge Bell presented to The Ten on 1 February 2001.

[2]Dumas Malone, *Jefferson and His Time*, 6 vols. (Boston: Little, Brown, 1948–1981).

I was attracted to the idea of knowing more about Jefferson's religious beliefs by chancing upon a copy of *The Jefferson Bible* on an occasion when I was visiting at Monticello.

I had often read that Jefferson had unusual religious beliefs, and it was said by many of his contemporaries that he was not a Christian. The so-called *Jefferson Bible* was a listing done by Jefferson of those parts of the Gospels which rested on the sayings of Jesus. Jefferson the thinker was searching for truth based on what Jesus said rather than what others wrote, and he particularly thought that Paul has distorted Christianity. Jefferson was not attracted to those things that could not be proven, such as the Virgin Birth and the Resurrection.

Jefferson did, however, have a strong belief in Jesus and his teachings and viewed him as the greatest example of man and his ethics in the history of mankind.

One must approach any study of Jefferson with the thought in mind that he was almost in a class by himself when it came to great thoughts about humanity. He died on 4 July 1826 at age 83, exactly fifty years from the time of the Declaration of Independence. (President John Adams died on the same day.)

Jefferson was invited to Washington to celebrate the Fourth of July that year but declined because of his failing health. However, he did write a letter to be published on that day. In the letter, he expressed the hope and belief that the bold action of the Declaration of Independence would be a signal to the world which would arouse men everywhere to throw off the shackles of tyranny and superstition and assume the blessings of self government. He said:

> All eyes are opened, or opening, to the rights of man. The general spread of the light of science has already laid open to every view the palpable truth, that the mass of mankind has not been born with saddles on their backs, not a favored few

booted and spurred ready to ride them legitimately, by the grace of God.[3]

Jefferson's biographer, Dr. Dumas Malone, in the closing paragraph of the last volume of his great biography, *The Sage of Monticello*, said of Jefferson:

> He has been viewed in his own time and circumstances. He was limited by these, and he made concessions to the society in which he lived. But he perceived eternal values and supported timeless causes. Thus, he became one of the most notable champions of freedom and enlightenment in recorded history.[4]

This champion of freedom and enlightenment had come to the view years earlier that it was not good to have a state religion. He championed breaking Virginia away from its state religion, the Church of England. He thought it better to have many different types of religious sects than one. He further thought that the Congregationalist Church of New England was almost a state religion, and he believed that freedom could not fully exist where religion and government were combined. Thus he authored the Virginia statute for religious freedom. It was this accomplishment and only two others—the Declaration of Independence and the founding of the University of Virginia—that he wanted noted on his tomb.

Jefferson believed that religion was a private matter, and he would not discuss his own religious views publicly. He was called an infidel by some and an agnostic by others, although he was a member of the Episcopal Church and de-

---

[3]Jefferson to Roger C. Weightman, Monticello, 24 June 1826. (This was the last letter Jefferson penned.) A copy of the letter is posted online at <http://www.let.rug.nl/use/P/tj3/writings/brf/jefl288.htm>.

[4]Malone, *The Sage of Monticello*, vol. 6 of *Jefferson and His Time* (Boston: Little, Brown, 1981).

signed the church in Charlottesville where his funeral took place. He also supported some Presbyterian and Baptist churches.

Jefferson feared the Presbyterians next to the Church of England, apparently believing that the Presbyterians were akin to a state religion. This must be viewed in the face of the fact that there were so many Scotch-Irish in the Southern region of the United State during his lifetime, and most of them were Presbyterians.

The public side of Jefferson's religion is well known, but not as much is known about his own particular religious beliefs. We turn now to explore his faith for whatever it was and whatever may have been its depth.

The letters between President John Adams and Jefferson are a good frame of reference, and we may begin with what each of them had to say about religion in their latter days.

Jefferson said that he would discuss religion only in the presence of reasonable company. He said that his religion was known only to himself and God and that its evidence must be sought in his life. "If that has been honest and dutiful to society," he said, "the religion which has regulated it cannot be a bad one."

Dr. Malone thought that Jefferson's view of religion and Adams's were the same. In one letter, Jefferson went to some length in giving his reason to Adams for believing in God. He rejected as false John Calvin's God, whom he regarded as cruel. The God that he and Adams adored, according to Dr. Malone, was the "Creator and benevolent governor of the world." To Jefferson's mind, it was impossible to view the universe without perceiving in it a designing mind and a guiding hand. He did not need revelation; to him the evidence was irresistible.

Jefferson never explained his belief in immortality, but often referred to it by saying that he would be reunited after death with his loved ones. Although John Adams shared Jefferson's faith, he made a humorous reference to it when he said that he hoped and believed that he and Jefferson would meet in another world, but if they did not, they would never know of it.

Adams knew that Jefferson was against clericalism and that he was dissatisfied with traditional Christian doctrine. He knew that Jefferson had his own version of the Gospels, although he never saw the version. In final form, Jefferson's version was called "The Life and Morals of Jesus of Nazareth," now known as *The Jefferson Bible*.[5] In his Bible, Jefferson deleted all of the passages having to do with miracles and arranged the balance of the text in four columns, in Greek, Latin, English, and French. Then he presented the teachings of Jesus in all of their purity.

Dr. Malone thinks that it was doubtful that anyone saw this work during Jefferson's lifetime. It was begun by Jefferson while he was president and was completed over several years. Dr. Malone concluded that in theology Jefferson was more of a Unitarian but not a sectarian, as such.

Jefferson suggested at one point that certain sectarian schools of divinity should be established on the confines of the University of Virginia to have the benefit of its facilities and instruction but not be a part of the University. He said that no subject was so important to every human being or so incumbent on him to study and investigate as were relations with his Maker and the duties arising from them. His thought was that the lack of instruction in the creeds of the various faiths in the state had created a "chasm" in the field of

---

[5]For example, *The Jefferson Bible: The Life and Morals of Jesus of Nazareth*, with an introduction by F. Forrester Church and an afterword by Jaroslav Pelikan (Boston: Becaon Press, 1989) based on the U.S. Government Printing Office version of 1904.

learning and that the University could help the schools of divinity in studying the various religions and would thus round out the circle of useful sciences in the University.

This was in keeping with Jefferson's view of academic freedom, where he once said of the University of Virginia, "This institution will be based on the illimitable freedom of the human mind. For here we are not afraid to follow truth wherever it may lead, nor to tolerate any error so long as reason is left free to combat it."

Dr. Malone deals with Jefferson the humanist at one point in his biography. He noted that Jefferson was a student of the moralists of Greek and Rome but that Jefferson thought their benevolence was too restricted as compared to what he perceived to be the ethics of Jesus. He thought that the teachings of Jesus on benevolence were of a fullness and sublimity never attained by a classical moralist. Dr. Malone said that until the end of his days, Jefferson remained anti-clerical and anti-doctrinal, but he regarded himself as a Christian.

In *Jefferson the President, First Term, 1801–1805*, volume 4 of *Jefferson and His Time*, Dr. Malone has a chapter entitled "The Religion of a Reasonable Man." In this chapter, Malone relates that Jefferson's political foes during the presidential campaign of 1800 had frequently denounced him in the press and pulpit as an atheist. Malone said that these name callers did not bother to define their term with precision, and they assumed that God was on their side in a conflict to which many mundane considerations entered. He said that at the same time there were always clergymen of the less-favored sects who supported Jefferson, and these were generally outside of New England.

Jefferson was urged before his inauguration to make a public avowal of his religious beliefs and to show that he was not hostile to the Christian religion. He refused to do so on the ground that his religion was a strictly private matter; but in his inaugural address, he did refer to religion in the following words:

> [E]nlightened by a benign religion, professed, indeed, and practiced in various forms, yet all of them inculcating honesty, truth, temperance, gratitude, and the love of man; acknowledging and adoring an overruling Providence, which by all its dispensations proves that it delights in the happiness of man here and his greater happiness hereafter. . . . [6]

The congregations in New England continued to refer to Jefferson as Anti-Christ, and it was generally thought that this hostility was really caused by Jefferson's insistence that there be a complete separation of church and state. And there was no doubt that the Jeffersonian philosophy was disquieting to some. For example, in his *Notes on the State of Virginia*, the only full-length book Jefferson ever authored, he said

> The legitimate powers of government extend to such acts only as are injurious to others. But it does me no injury for my neighbor to say there are twenty gods or no God. [7]

Furthermore, Jefferson's 1779 draft of a bill which, with very little revision, in 1786 became "The Virginia Act for Establishing Religious Freedom," provided

> that no man shall be compelled to frequent or support any religious Worship place or Ministry whatsoever, nor shall be enforced, restrained, molested, or burthened in his body or goods, nor shall otherwise suffer on account of his religious opinions or belief, but that all men shall be free to profess, and

---

[6]Jefferson, "First Inaugural Address," Wednesday 4 March 1801, Senate document 101-10 (U.S.G.P.O., 1989) as posted online at <http://www.bartrleby.com/124/pres16.html>.

[7]"The Different Religions Received into That State," *Notes on the State of Virginia* (London: J. Stockdale, 1787) 285.

by argument to maintain their opinions in matters of religion, and that the same shall in no wise diminish, enlarge, or affect their civil capacities.[8]

Thus, while he was not an atheist, his views conflicted with those who had various views as to the true way to salvation, whether they were Congregational, Baptist, Catholic, or any other church. His fault, then—if fault it was—was that he thought there was room in our country for those with varying views of religion, including those who had no religion.

This brings us back to the observation that the dominant theme of Jefferson's life was that of a political philosopher based on the maximum freedom that could be afforded to the citizen in a democracy. His views were pluralistic—he thought that a multiplicity of religious sects was desirable, seeing safety against tyranny in numbers. It was difficult to say that he was anti-religion since he attacked no group on religious grounds. He, in fact, had been a generous contributor to churches and made a special point of attending divine services while he was president.

Jefferson's problem with his opponents was that he did not care for ceremony in the Church and that he abhorred mystery in anything that he regarded as obfuscation. The God he worshiped was the God of Nature. Viewing the Great Creator with an awe and reverence beyond most, he sought with "rare diligence," in the words of Dr. Malone, to discover and obey His laws. To Jefferson, there was no field or area that the mind might not and should not freely examine, and he himself would accept only what had gained the sanction of his critical and enlightened intelligence. It was no wonder that

---

[8]Jefferson, "A Bill for Establishing Religious Freedom," 12 June 1779, in *The Papers of Thomas Jefferson*, 33 vols., ed. Julian P. Boyd et al (Princeton NJ: Princeton University Press, 1950ff.) 2:304.

some devout men with comparable faith and human intelligence, but with more devotion to inherited tradition, should have been disquieted by Jefferson.

Jefferson's Bible demonstrated his deep admiration for the doctrines of Jesus, because to him Jesus' teachings gave clear meaning to the attributes and providence of God, and he approved Jesus' emphasis on the future life as a motive to moral conduct. He thought that the teachings of Jesus brought about an inculcation of "universal philanthropy, not only to kindred and friends, to neighbors and countrymen, but to all mankind." Dr. Malone said of this that Jefferson was brushing aside the trappings of ceremony and the obscuring mantle of theology and that he had arrived at the heart of the matter.

At one point, Jefferson wrote his friend, the Philadelphia physician Dr. Benjamin Rush, that as a result of a life of inquiry and reflection he was not opposed to the general precepts of Jesus himself. He thought that others in their writings had corrupted Christianity, but he said, "I am a Christian, sincerely attached to his doctrines in preface to all others and ascribing to Jesus every human excellence."

Whether others agreed with Jefferson that he was a Christian was subject to debate then, as it is now. One of his minister friends was surprised at Jefferson's opinion that Jesus never laid claim to a divine mission and wrote him at length on the subject to provide him with further food for thought. Dr. Rush thought that, whatever Jefferson's views, the only test God would apply at the judgment seat was that of conduct. According to Dr. Malone, Rush, along with Jefferson, could have quoted Pope's familiar lines:

> For modes of faith, let graceless zealots fight;
> His can't be wrong whose life is in the right;

In faith and hope the world will disagree,
But all mankind's concern is charity.[9]

What conclusion do we reach? A scholarly Unitarian clergyman, Henry Wilder Foot, wrote in the middle of the twentieth century that Jefferson's "knowledge and admiration of the teachings of Jesus have never been equaled by any other president."

Jefferson did not call himself a Unitarian until he was in his extreme old age, but he apparently reached that conclusion himself. Jefferson's faith did not rest on a belief in the divinity of Jesus or in the Virgin Birth and the Resurrection, but rather on the conviction that Nature was proof enough of God and that all live by God's plan. Perhaps some would say this is a Unitarian belief. It is Deist, at least. But Jefferson, as an apostle of spiritual freedom, regarded himself as a Christian.

It was well put by Dr. Malone that Jefferson had the religion of a reasonable man. Perhaps he was not a Christian as most would define that term, but he was not antireligious, and he had a faith of his own. As the "father" of the Virginia Act for Establishing Religious Freedom, and in his own reluctance to share his personal beliefs for political purposes, Thomas Jefferson was the leading champion of religious freedom.

---

[9]Alexander Pope, "Of the Nature and State of Man with Respect to Society," epistle III (1733) of *Essay on Man* (1732, 1733, 1744).

Chapter 6

The Trial of Aaron Burr

A Triumph of the American Justice System [1]

Aaron Burr served as vice president of our country during the years 1801–1805 under President Thomas Jefferson. Jefferson did not offer Burr a place during his second term, and his adventures that led to his trial for treason ensued in the years immediately thereafter.

Aaron Burr, Jr. was born in 1756 in Newark, New Jersey. He was the son of Aaron Burr, Sr., the second president of the College of New Jersey (now Princeton University) and the grandson of Jonathan Edwards, another president of the College of New Jersey. Burr entered college at the age of thirteen and graduated at the age of sixteen. He was a Revolutionary War hero, rising to the rank of lieutenant colonel at the age of twenty-one.

After the Revolution, Burr became an excellent attorney in New York City. In 1789, the year George Washington took office as our first president, Burr was appointed attorney general of New York. Two years later, he was elected to the Senate from New York.

He was not liked by George Washington or by Thomas Jefferson, although Washington and Jefferson did not like each other either. To complete the trilogy, Jefferson and Alexander Hamilton were enemies—at least in political philosophy. Burr and Hamilton became great enemies, and this led to Hamilton's death and Burr's downfall.

---

[1]Editor's note. Judge Bell presented this account to The Ten on 2 December 1999.

In 1796, Burr ran for vice president with Thomas Jefferson, and they lost to John Adams. But Adams's vice president was Thomas Jefferson, who had the second most electoral votes—the way vice presidents were elected at the time. In the election of 1800, both Jefferson and Burr ran for president and received the same number of electoral votes. The election then went to the House of Representatives to break the tie. Jefferson prevailed to become president with Burr becoming vice president.

Hoping to rebuild his political fortunes after knowing that he would be dropped from what was then called the Democratic-Republican ticket for the 1804 election with President Jefferson, in 1804 Burr ran a losing race for Governor of New York. This was while still serving as vice president. Hamilton also lived in New York, and he did everything he could to defeat Burr. Some of Hamilton's derogatory comments, which were apparently personal in nature, appeared in print. Burr demanded a retraction, which Hamilton refused to make. Burr then challenged him to a duel.

The duel took place in New Jersey on 11 July 1804, again while Burr was serving as vice president. Hamilton was shot after he apparently misfired at Burr—some said by design. Hamilton died shortly thereafter, and Burr was charged with murder. He fled to Pennsylvania to escape arrest and continued to serve out the final months of his term as vice president. It was said that he handled his duties well as vice president and he presided over the impeachment trial of Justice Samuel Chase during this period.

Upon leaving the vice presidency, Burr became involved in an undertaking to create an empire of some kind in the territory between the Ohio River and Mexico. But it was never clear just how the territory would come to be—whether to invade Mexico or the New Orleans area or to cause the Mississippi Territory, and perhaps Kentucky, to leave the

Union and become a separate country. Burr had a handful of followers and a coconspirator, General James Wilkinson, the highest ranking general in the United States Army. Wilkinson was in charge of the American military forces in the Louisiana Territory, which included the New Orleans area, formerly under lease from Spain.

On 11 March 1805, in addition to his other duties as general, Wilkinson became governor of the Louisiana Territory by appointment of President Jefferson. He was replaced as governor by Meriwether Lewis on 3 March 1807. Lewis died under mysterious circumstances, thought by some to have a Wilkinson connection.

Wilkinson, it later developed from Spanish archives identifying "Agent 13," was on the Spanish payroll for many years, as a double agent, in fact, although he was a great friend of Washington, Adams, and Jefferson. As will be seen, he may have been America's first triple agent. He was an American general, a paid secret agent of Spain, and then perhaps used by Jefferson against Spain in the hope of acquiring the Florida Territory from Spain.

At the most, Burr had only a few people in his group. He operated out of Blennerhassett Island, an island in the Ohio River owned by one of his alleged coconspirators, Harman Blennerhassett, a wealthy Irish-American lawyer who apparently had agreed to bankroll Burr's scheme and had offered his island as a "secret" headquarters and staging area. Burr claimed he would have many followers once his expedition south commenced.

General Wilkinson was in the thick of whatever it was that Burr was planning, but he reported the conspiracy to Jefferson so as to absolve himself of any charges. Wilkinson's letter was received by Jefferson on 25 November 1806, but was dated 21 October 1806.

Jefferson ordered the arrest of Burr, and Burr surrendered in the Mississippi Territory. He was taken to the city of Washington, near Natchez in the Mississippi Territory, for trial for alleged treason. The grand jury there refused to charge him but kept him under bond for the misdemeanor charge of leading an invasion of Mexico. He left that jurisdiction without permission and was then arrested by the army pursuant to orders from General Wilkinson. He was en route to Washington (D.C.) under guard and had reached Fredericksburg, Virginia, when orders were received to take him to Richmond, Virginia for trial. This directive came from President Jefferson, who had publicly stated that Burr was guilty of treason.

Jurisdiction was based in the federal court in Richmond because Blennerhassett Island—from which Burr and his coconspirators had been operating—was in Wood County, Virginia (now in West Virginia), in the territory of the Fifth Circuit federal court, of which Virginia was then a part.

After a sharply contested grand jury proceeding, Burr was charged with treason. Oddly, General Wilkinson was almost indicted by the same grand jury by a vote of 13 to 12—which indicates the low regard in which Wilkinson was held by some of the grand jurors, including the foreman, John Randolph of Roanoke, then a member of Congress.

The trial then took place in the United States District Court in Richmond. There was a duly appointed and sitting judge, Cyrus Griffin, but he was joined, as was proper at the time, by the chief justice of the Supreme Court, John Marshall, the circuit justice who actually chose to preside at the trial.

From a historical perspective, an important precedent was created in this case with respect to presidential power and status. It was the response to a subpoena issued to President Jefferson to produce the letter to Jefferson from General

Wilkinson for the trial. General Wilkinson had been called as a witness. Wilkinson, a suspect character, was used by the defense as the foil in the defense of Burr.

To add to the high drama of the trial, Justice Marshall and President Jefferson were cousins, but were political enemies, Marshall being a Federalist and Jefferson being a Republican (later known as Democrat-Republican and now the Democratic Party). Marshall opined that President Jefferson could be called as a witness, that he was not a king, and thus he had to produce the letter.

Despite President Jefferson's active pursuit of him, Burr was able to assemble a potent group of lawyers in his defense. Burr's lawyers included Edmond Randolph, our first attorney general, and Charles Lee, a former attorney general under Presidents Washington and Adams, along with John Wickham, Benjamin Botts, and John Baker, all prominent Virginia lawyers. Burr's defense also included Luther Martin of Baltimore, who had successfully represented Justice Chase at his impeachment trial, which was also a prosecution at the instance of President Jefferson. He had been attorney general of Maryland.

Martin was a firebrand type of lawyer who kept a jug of whiskey at the counsel table. Whether the whiskey made him more vigorous is not known, but he was indeed vigorous. He was well known to Jefferson as a political enemy and legal antagonist. Jefferson once described him as a legal bulldog.

The prosecution included Caesar A. Rodney, the attorney general of the United States (then a part-time position) in the earlier part of the case; but Rodney dropped from sight, some think because his father knew that General Wilkinson, the principal witness against Burr, was a scoundrel. The prosecution was then under the direction of the United States Attorney for Virginia, George Hay, assisted by William Wirt (later attorney general under Presidents Monroe and John Quincy Adams) as well as Alexander McRae, a Richmond lawyer.

The burden of proof on the prosecution and the skullduggery of General Wilkinson were the key points in the trial.

It was known that Wilkinson had written letters to Jefferson about Burr, and Martin conceived the idea of serving a subpoena on President Jefferson to obtain these letters. There was some doubt amongst counsel as to whether the president could be subpoenaed, but Martin prevailed and Jefferson was subpoenaed. This was the first instance in the history of our country where the president was subpoenaed.

Jefferson, with some misgivings, concluded that he had to respond to the subpoena. So he asked the attorney general to work out an arrangement where he could send the letters without having to appear himself, and this was done.

Now a word about General Wilkinson, the ranking general in the United States Army at the time and an officer under Washington during the Revolution. He lost out in the Army by participating in the so-called "Conway Cabal," which was a failed conspiracy to replace General George Washington with General Gates. Wilkinson became a land speculator in Kentucky after the War and then worked himself back into the Army as a career officer. In 1791, he was inherited by Jefferson from Adams, who inherited him from Washington.

Rumors about Wilkinson's connection to Spain reached Washington, Adams, and Jefferson, but they discounted them amidst such rumors about many others in the Western Territories.[2]

---

[2]For more on Wilkinson's duplicity (triplicity?) see Walter R. Borneman, *1812. The War That Forged a Nation* (New York: HarperCollins, 2004).

Under Jefferson, Wilkinson was headquartered in the New Orleans Territory, which was adjacent to the Mississippi Territory and south of the Louisiana Territory. Jefferson declined to make him governor of the Louisiana Territory on the ground of not mixing military and civil authority.

Early in his second term and before the Burr trial, Jefferson did give General Wilkinson the additional duty of governor of the Louisiana Territory. He later said he thought of the Louisiana Territory as a military outpost and hence there was no mixing of military and civil authority. All in all, Wilkinson was a man of great but corrupt power—as was demonstrated by his conspiring with Burr, then turning Burr in to Jefferson, and later arresting Burr and several of Burr's accomplices. Wilkinson sent at least two of them under army arrest back to Washington for trial (Bollman and Swartwout, to be mentioned below) and ordered Burr sent first to Mississippi and then to Richmond after there was no indictment of Burr in Mississippi. Wilkinson was, factually, the most important witness against Burr, although it was his hope to be a witness in absentia.

Another event must be mentioned in connection with the Burr trial, and that is the impeachment trial of Justice Samuel Chase in 1804–1805. It was Jefferson's view that he had defeated the Federalists, but they had held onto the federal judgeships. Jefferson said that the Federalists had "retired into the judiciary as a stronghold. There the remains of federalism are preserved and fed from the treasury, and from that battery all of the works of republicanism are beaten down and erased."[3]

---

[3]Jefferson, in a letter (1801) to John Dickinson, as recorded in *The Jeffersonian Cyclopedia; a Comprehensive Collection of the Views of Thomas Jefferson*, ed. John P. Foley (New York and London: Funk & Wagnalls, 1900) 330b.

Jefferson was not at the Constitutional Convention, and it was his decided belief that the Constitution gave federal judges too much power. He believed the Constitution should be amended to allow removal of federal judges by vote of the Congress with the approval of the president. Out of this feeling came the effort to impeach federal judges, including Justice Chase. Chase was acquitted by the Senate, and thereafter Jefferson viewed the impeachment procedure as a charade.

The case against Justice Chase in the main was based on a charge he gave to a grand jury in Baltimore. (A part of the duty of justices at the time was to charge grand juries.) In the charge, Chase had railed against universal suffrage and predicted loss of property and personal liberty and a mobocracy government. This was an allusion to Jefferson's views, but the issue was the justice's freedom of speech. The vote on this count in the bill of impeachment was the heaviest vote against Chase: 19 for conviction and 15 against, thus short of the two-thirds necessary for conviction.

The charges in the Chase trial tie into Jefferson's advocacy role in it and in Burr's trial. Some of the lawyers for Chase also defended Burr, particularly former Attorney General Charles Lee and Luther Martin. John Randolph, the speaker of the House at the time of the Chase trial, was the prosecutor. He was later the foreman of the Burr grand jury in Richmond and sought the indictment of Wilkinson.

Chase was acquitted by the Senate on 1 March 1805, as the last order of business in the Senate in the first term of Jefferson. It was the last function of Burr, who, as vice president and thus president of the Senate, presided at the trial and then concluded his service with an extraordinary farewell address. (The Constitution, art. 1, sec. 3(6) provides that the chief justice of the Supreme Court shall preside in any impeachment trial of the president, but not so with judges.)

Burr received plaudits for his impartiality in the Chase proceedings.

There is one last matter to be mentioned that bears heavily on the Burr trial. Wilkinson had ordered the arrests of two of Burr's accomplices, Erick Bollman and Samuel Swartwout, in New Orleans, and sent them under guard some 2,000 miles to Washington, D.C. Their motions for release on petitions for the writ of habeas corpus were granted, prior to the Burr trial, by the Supreme Court in an opinion by Chief Justice Marshall. A number of the lawyers who appeared for Justice Chase and later for Burr were in these habeas cases. Attorney General Rodney appeared for the government.

The principal evidence against these defendants was a report by Wilkinson of the substance of a letter from Burr to Wilkinson. This was offered as proof of the treason. This was a part of the affidavit given by Wilkinson in causing the arrest of the defendants.

Chief Justice Marshall said that there had to be proof that war had been levied against the United States.

The Jefferson forces relied on this language to connect Burr in his trial to the treason, apparently overlooking that part of the opinion that the prosecution had the burden of proving that men were actually assembled for the treasonable purpose explained further in the opinion, "as assembling for the purpose of executing a treasonable design." The order of the Supreme Court was to release Bollman and Swartwout for lack of sufficient evidence of levying war.

Justice Marshall's ruling was that Burr was not present at Blennerhassett Island, where the assembly to levy war took place; that to prove that he nevertheless participated constructively in the assembly required proof by two witnesses of the assembly for the purpose of levying war. There was no such proof, and absent such, proof of circumstantial facts would not be allowed.

Burr's acquittal did not end his troubles. The jury also acquitted him of the misdemeanor charge of preparing to invade Mexico, but the prosecution, at the instance of President Jefferson, ordered Burr put under bond so that he could be prosecuted in Ohio for the same misdemeanor. There was such an indictment, but it was never pursued.

There were no winners in this unfortunate affair. It ended Burr's public career. He lived for another thirty years, outliving Jefferson and Wilkinson, but he never again rose to prominence of any kind.

Jefferson served out his second term. His reputation suffered because of his partisan and dictatorial conduct toward Chase and Burr while accomplishing little. John Adams criticized him for announcing Burr's guilt before his trial. Andrew Jackson observed that Jefferson learned from the French to cut off a man's head because he didn't agree with him.

Wilkinson died in Mexico after having been relieved of his Army service by President Madison, who said that Wilkinson was the legacy of Jefferson.

Dr. Dumas Malone, Jefferson's biographer, suggested that Jefferson was using Wilkinson against the Spanish, although he knew that Wilkinson had been and was then a Spanish agent, thus making Wilkinson into a "triple agent"—for the U.S., for Spain against the U.S., and then for the U.S. against Spain. The Spanish Archives later disclosed that he was "Spanish Agent No. 13" and was on the Spanish payroll for many years. No greater traitor can be imagined.

The Burr episode was not one of our nation's proudest moments, except for the pride that we should have in our justice system.

Chapter 7

Joshua Lawrence Chamberlain: Scholar and Warrior

Duty [1]

Joshua Lawrence Chamberlain (1828–1914) was among the best-educated soldiers in the Union Army, if not the best. He was a graduate of Bowdoin College in Brunswick, Maine, studied for the ministry, and ended up teaching at Bowdoin. He had mastered a number of languages, including Greek and German. His teaching subjects were Religion, then Rhetoric and Oratory, which was followed by Modern Languages.

He answered the call to the colors in 1862 and enlisted in the Twentieth Maine Regiment. He received the rank of Lieutenant Colonel. The Twentieth Maine became part of the legendary First Infantry Division with its flag of a red Maltese cross on a white background, perhaps the most storied division in Army history.

The Twentieth Maine and Joshua Chamberlain went through twenty-four battles together, from Antietam to Appomattox. Chamberlain was wounded six times, once severely, and he suffered from this wound for the rest of his life, although he lived some fifty years after receiving the wound. He was given up for dead at the time of this wound and was saved by what was called, at the time, a medical miracle in surgery. He was taken to City Point, Virginia, some sixteen miles from where he was wounded at Petersburg, for additional surgery and then by boat to the U.S. Naval

---

[1]Editor's note. Judge Bell presented this paper to The Ten on 27 March 1996.

Academy Hospital at Annapolis. He was wounded in May 1864 and was back on duty in September. The wound he suffered was from a miniball, which entered near one hip and exited near the other hip.

Joshua Chamberlain was best known in the war for his defense of Little Round Top on the first day of the Battle of Gettysburg on 2 July 1863, the turning point of the Civil War. After fighting down to hardly any ammunition, and despite wounds to himself, he gave the order to charge with bayonets, and the charge broke the attack of the Southern forces on Little Round Top. Absent holding Little Round Top, the Union forces would have been enveloped by the Confederate operation which was seeking to sweep to the right around Little Round Top and circle back left, to capture or thoroughly defeat the Union Army. This operation was a military necessity, inasmuch as the Confederates allowed all of the high ground at Gettysburg to be occupied by the Union forces. Heretofore, particularly at Fredericksburg, the Confederates had always seized the high ground and forced the Union Army to advance on them, thereby inflicting heavy losses.

The bravery of Chamberlain, then a full colonel, at Little Round Top was noted, and he was recommended for promotion to Brigadier General, but he was neither decorated nor promoted at the time. Many years later, he was given the Congressional Medal of Honor for his activities at Little Round Top as well as on the third day of Gettysburg in the face of Pickett's charge. However, he was not promoted until almost a year later in the Battle of Petersburg, when General Grant ordered him promoted, on the spot, to Brigadier General. His promotion was affirmed in Washington by the War Department and by the Senate. By the time of the surrender at Appomattox, he had been promoted to Major General.

The most remarkable event from the standpoint of nation-hood and humaneness in the life of General Chamberlain occurred as part of the surrender ceremony at Appomattox.

In his book, *The Passing of the Armies*, General Chamberlain professed not to know how he was selected to command the honor guard during the surrender ceremonies. By this time, Chamberlain was in the Fifth Corps of the Army of the Potomac under General Griffin, who told him that he was to command the honor guard. Chamberlain was a favorite of Grant, another warrior type, and it may be surmised that Grant approved the selection. In the three days following the surrender, the process of dismantling the Confederate cavalry, artillery, and infantry was taking place. Meanwhile, there was much mingling among the troops and other evidence of good spirit. Lee's cavalry and artillery were the first to be dismantled, leaving the infantry for last, and to be the subject of the surrender ceremony.

The Southern forces in the ceremony were commanded by General John B. Gordon of Georgia. With permission from no one and without discussing it with anyone of high rank, Chamberlain decided to have his command give the traditional military salute to the fallen Confederate troops. As Chamberlain later wrote:

> The momentous meaning of this occasion impressed me deeply. I resolved to mark it by some token of recognition, which could be no other than a salute of arms. Well aware of the responsibility assumed, and of the criticisms that would follow, as the sequel proved, nothing of that kind could move me in the least. The act could be defended, if needful, by the suggestion that such a salute was not to the cause for which the flag of the Confederacy stood, but to its going down before the flag of the Union. My main reason, however, was one for which I sought no authority nor asked forgiveness. Before us in proud humiliation stood the embodiment of manhood: men

for whom neither toils and sufferings, nor the fact of death, nor disaster, nor hopelessness could bend from their resolve; standing before us now, thin, worn, and famished, but erect, and with eyes looking level into ours, walking memories that bound us together as no other bond;—was not such manhood to be welcomed back into a Union so tested and assured?[2]

The salute was given in a military parade, a part of which included the Confederates stacking their arms and surrendering their flags. It was a moving ceremony, and Gordon, as a part of the ceremony, again without preplanning, commanded his troops to return the salute, so there was a salute by the North to the South and from the South back to the North, all as professional soldiers on both sides were able to do. The salute, one to another, was in sharp contrast to what the civilian forces of the Northern reconstruction were able to do to the South in the years ahead.

All of the days at Appomattox were filled with emotion, beginning with the flag-of-truce approach by an officer from Gordon's division, saying that Lee had not been able to find Grant to respond to his request of surrender and that Lee intended to surrender and asked for a truce. This was the first information that Chamberlain had of a surrender. Grant was en route to Appomattox. This first courier came from Gordon's division, and shortly thereafter another flag of truce came, borne by an officer from Longstreet's headquarters. Chamberlain, with his own eyes, saw Lee riding Traveler to

---

[2]Chamberlain, *The Passing of the Armies: An Account of the Final Campaign of the Army of the Potomac, Based upon Personal Reminiscences of the First Army Corps* (Lincoln: University of Nebraska Press, 1998; first edition, New York and London: Putnam's, 1915) 260. This passage, in its entirety, is printed in the Appomattox Court House National Park section of *The Civil War Battlefield Guide* (New York: Houghton Mifflin, 1998).

Appomattox, when he passed through Chamberlain's lines. Shortly thereafter, he also saw General Grant passing through en route to Appomattox.

We move from the surrender at Appomattox on through Lincoln's assassination on 14 April 1865 and the grand parade of victory in Washington to the impeachment trial of President Johnson in 1868. Chamberlain was, by that time, the governor of Maine.

Senator Fessenden, one of the Senators from Maine, was one of the seven Republicans who voted not to impeach President Johnson and, because of that, Fessenden came under heavy attack in Maine. Chamberlain defended him strongly. Also, Chamberlain thought there ought to be some delay in extending the vote to the former slaves. This was definitely the minority view in Maine. Some of this may have been caused by Chamberlain's having to put down black rioters in the Petersburg, Virginia vicinity while he was taking his troops back to Washington for the grand parade.

In addition to being governor of Maine for four years, General Chamberlain became president of Bowdoin College for several years. He had gone back to Bowdoin to teach upon his discharge from the military, but he left in less than a year to become governor.

Like many high generals in both armies, General Chamberlain had business interests in the railroad industry and in real estate. At one time, he was developing land near the Homosassa River in Florida, between Homosassa and Ocala. Like many others as well, he finally ended up with a government job as surveyor of the port of Portland, Maine, something of a sinecure during his old age.

Chamberlain spent his post-Civil War years ahead of public opinion. As noted, he was against the Reconstruction and viewed the impeachment of President Johnson as "the great American farce." His years as governor went well. The governor's term of office was only one year and he served four years. His years as president of Bowdoin College were frustrating. He wanted to modernize the curriculum, which his trustees always thought could not be done because of the expense.

He was for the death penalty in Maine, though it was later abolished. While governor, he refused to mitigate the sentence of death to a rapist who also murdered his victims. The attorney general of the state wanted to mitigate the sentence of death and the anti-capital punishment adherents were likewise agitating. Chamberlain said:

> If a person can be convicted of capital crime by evidence given under the pressure of his consummate hope of reward, then the altar of justice is no longer the asylum of justice, and life and liberty must seek some other defense.[3]

This was his answer to the attorney general who rested his mitigation argument on the idea that the convicted man had "turned state's evidence." Chamberlain said that the attorney general had every opportunity to mitigate by withdrawing portions of the indictment in token of the service rendered. He noted that neither the jury nor the judge, after sentence, had recommended the convicted man to the mercy of the governor.

As to capital punishment generally, he said that the consideration of public safety convinced him that it was not time to soften penalties. He said:

> Too much crime is abroad, and emboldened by the mildness and uncertainty of punishment—mercy is indeed a heavenly grace—but it should not be shown to crime. It is the crime and

---

[3]As recently recorded in *Joshua Chamberlain: A Hero's Life and Legacy*, by John J. Pullen (Mechanicsburg PA: Stackpole Books, 1999) 43.

not the man at which the law strikes. It is not to prevent the man, alone, from repeating his offense, but to prevent others from so doing.

In his own reflections on the Civil War and in his activities following the War, Chamberlain visited Gettysburg on at least two occasions and went to many reunions of the Northern forces, to others where veterans of both sides attended, and kept up with his friends from the Army days.

He thought often of his friend and commander, General Griffin, who died within two years after the war, while on duty in Texas, from yellow fever. During the Washington ceremonies following the Appomattox surrender, Chamberlain and other members of the First Infantry Division had presented General Griffin with a jeweled battle flag in miniature of the red Maltese Cross on the white background. In accepting the miniature, General Griffin said to Chamberlain,

> You, yourself, General, a youthful subordinate when I first took command of this division, now through so many deep experiences risen to be its tested, trusted and beloved commander—you are an example of what experiences of loyalty and fortitude, of change and constancy, have marked the career of this honored division.[4]

Years after the war, Chamberlain remembered passing near Fredericksburg, en route to Washington after Appomattox. His forces bivouacked on the night of 9 May 1865 near Fredericksburg. Private Gerrish of the 20th Maine is said to have written of that night that he walked past a little church once filled with screaming, groaning wounded, but now he heard only the strains of a familiar hymn, "Jesus, Lover of My Soul." Private Gerrish found the breastworks on Marye's Heights leveled, and the green grass covering all. He said that

---

[4]As quoted by Chamberlain in *The Passing of the Armies*, 324.

the night was soft and balmy, and he heard the tinkle of a cowbell in a distant field and the voices of children playing in a yard below him. As he thought of the war, now over, of the comrades who had perished on these very slopes in the roar of battle, where the South had the high ground, he found the place and the silence oppressive and hurried back to the bivouac.

Chamberlain recalled, with sadness, those slopes once so heavily flecked with blue, that dreadful day of the Army's life two-and-a-half years ago, and he thought, "What years and with what changes of men as if to place the seal of tragedy on the field." Chamberlain thought that it was all part of a brave but melancholy past. As author Wallace said in the *Soul of the Lion*:

> This former theological student and professor of Religion and Modern Languages at Bowdoin College was, indeed, one of the most remarkable soldiers in the Union Army, combining to an extraordinary degree ability and valor.[5]

Chamberlain, in later years, said that he disagreed with General Sherman's statement that "War is Hell." He said that fighting and destruction are terrible, but are sometimes agencies of heavenly, rather than hellish, powers. As he said, "In the privations and sufferings endured, as well as the strenuous action of battle, some of the highest qualities of manhood are called forth—courage, self-command, sacrifice of self for the sake of something held higher."[6]

On one occasion, the students at his beloved Bowdoin College formally requested President Hyde of Bowdoin to advise General Chamberlain, in view of the approaching fifti-

---

[5]Willard Mosher Wallace, *Soul of a Lion. A Biography of General Joshua L. Chamberlain* (New York: T. Nelson, 1960).

[6]*The Passing of the Armies*, 385.

eth anniversary of the Battle of Gettysburg, of their gratitude for his service. At an assembly in the chapel, President Hyde said in a presentation to Chamberlain:

> [Your students], which you left to obey your Country's call and to which you returned after years of heroic and victorious service, by rising vote, have requested me to express to you and the brave men who fought with you in the great cause, their gratitude for the privilege of living in a country undivided by secession and unstained by slavery; and to assure you that your noble example will ever be an incentive to the lives of patriotic service, in peace so long as honorable peace is possible; in war whenever unavoidable and righteous war shall call.

Time was running out for the General. By this time, he spent most of his time in his government job, but he never lost interest in his books. His private library contained more than 2,000 volumes, many on the Civil War. In his library and study at Brunswick, Maine, just off the campus of Bowdoin College, in addition to the books, he had many mementoes of the war.

General Chamberlain died on 24 February 1914 at the age of eighty-five. In the end, he died from complications from his Civil War wounds. His funeral took place in Portland, Maine, followed by another service in Brunswick, where he was buried. Dr. Hyde perhaps captured the feeling in his address at the service in Brunswick. He gave an account of Chamberlain's life and pointed out that oftentimes Chamberlain had stood in advance of his time, as a reform-minded president of a college that did not have the money to afford the reforms, as a statesman who courageously opposed the leaders of his party when convinced that to comply with his wishes was to misuse the power which the people had given. He said of Chamberlain's actions at Appomattox in saluting the defeated troops of Lee, whom he looked upon as no longer enemies, but friends and fellow Americans, as a deed "in which military glory and Christian magnanimity were fused." President Hyde concluded:

> Whoever, whether as a patriot or a Christian, dares to plant his standards far in advance of present and sustained achievement, runs the risk of . . . misinterpretation. . . .

> [General Chamberlain] never hauled down his flag to the low level of what he or any man could easily do or habitually be. All [that] he said and did was bright and burning with an ardor of idealism which in the home was devotion; in the college was loyalty; in the state and nation was patriotism; toward humanity and God was religion.

As you may know, "Taps" was written by a Civil War Union soldier, Dan Butterfield. In *Soul of the Lion*, Wallace says:

> The funeral took place among the pines near Chamberlain's beloved college, the rifles volleyed in final salute, and the haunting notes of . . . "Taps" echoed through the cold winter air, [and] for those living who had loved Chamberlain, this was a moment of desolation. For the General, himself, it may well have been as at times he seems to have believed, only the continuation of a hazardous, but exhilarating journey.[7]

One might say of him, as John Bunyan wrote long ago, "so he passed over, and all the trumpets sounded for him on the other side."[8]

---

[7]Wallace, *Soul of the Lion.*

[8]John Bunyan, *The Pilgrim's Progress* (1678) pt. 2 ("Mr. Valiant-for-Truth").

Chapter 8

John Singleton Mosby: "The Gray Ghost"

Honor [1]

One of the legendary figures of the Civil War was a person not of high rank, John S. Mosby (1833–1916).[2] Mosby began as a private in 1861 and reached the rank of colonel in 1864. His first command was not until the winter of 1863 and consisted of only nine soldiers. Shortly thereafter, this force was increased to fifteen, and it became the nucleus for the 43rd Battalion, a part of Jeb Stuart's command in the Army of Northern Virginia.

The 43rd Battalion was in existence from 1 January 1863 to 21 April 1865 and was the foremost scouting and guerilla organization in the Army of Northern Virginia. By the time of the surrender of Lee at Appomattox, the Battalion consisted of eight companies divided into two parts, each under a major. To the Federal forces, it was at the top of the "most wanted" list of all organizations in the Army of Northern

---

[1]The Ten heard this paper from Judge Bell on 23 February 1995.

[2]The biography of Mosby, *Ranger Mosby*, by Virgil Carrington Jones (Chapel Hill: University of North Carolina Press, 1944) is an exciting account of Mosby's life and of his command. *Mosby's Rangers*, by Jeffry D. Wert (New York: Simon & Schuster, 1990) is no less informative and enjoyable. A number of other books have been written over the years about Mosby and the Rangers, several by members of the 43rd Battalion, and there is much on Mosby in *Lee's Lieutenants* (1942–1944). Mosby's papers are at the Library of Congress. The official records of the Union and Confederate armies compiled under the heading, *The War of the Rebellion: A Compilation of the Official Records of the Union and Confederate Armies* (70 vols., 1880–1901) contain much information on Mosby.

Virginia. Rewards were offered for Mosby's capture, and special forces were deployed to contain and destroy his command. Grant ordered that he be brought in "dead or alive."

Mosby was born in 1833 about forty miles west of Richmond at the home of his maternal grandfather. His mother had come home from Nelson County, Virginia, to give birth at the home of her father, James McLaurine. His mother's grandfather was a Scotch immigrant and an Episcopal minister who had come to America in 1750. He preached on Sunday and farmed during the week. Mosby's father, Alfred Daniel Mosby, was a graduate of Hampden Sydney College.

Not much is known of Mosby's life before he reached the University of Virginia. At one point during his childhood, his father moved from Nelson County into the adjoining county of Albermarle. Their new home was in the Blue Ridge Mountains, four miles from Charlottesville. John had been taught Latin and Greek and mathematics by two teachers who later served on the faculty of Washington College during the presidency of Robert E. Lee.

Mosby entered the University of Virginia in 1850, lived at home, and made a good record. He moved into a boarding house in Charlottesville beginning with his second year and was there until he was expelled in the spring of his senior year, when his violent nature surfaced.

Mosby shot a medical student when the student came to Mosby's boarding house. It turned out that the medical student was a bully and had been in trouble a number of times. He had threatened Mosby and then came looking for him. The student's wounds eventually healed, but Mosby was expelled from the university shortly before his graduation. He had been arrested after the shooting in March of 1854 and was held in jail until his arraignment and trial in May.

The facts before the jury were that earlier the medical student had almost killed one student with a pocket knife and

another student with a rock. Mosby himself apparently had
been in a fight during his freshman year with a town police-
man. The jury was deadlocked for two days, but reached a
verdict that Mosby was not guilty of the first count of the
indictment of malicious shooting, but that he was guilty of the
second count of unlawful shooting. He was sentenced to im-
prisonment in the county jail for twelve months and ordered
to pay a $500 fine.

A group of Mosby sympathizers started a movement to
have him pardoned and on 23 December 1854 Mosby walked
out free. The governor had granted him a pardon as a Christmas present, and the legislature rescinded the $500 fine at the
next session.

In his lifetime, good fortune often came to Mosby. While
in jail, he struck up a conversation with the prosecutor and
told him that he was determined to become a lawyer. The
prosecutor, William J. Robertson, later a justice of the Virginia Supreme Court and the first president of the Virginia
Bar Association, took Mosby at his word and sent him *Blackstone's Commentaries on the Law* and a volume of *Greenleaf
on Evidence* to study.

Mosby studied in Robertson's law office for several
months after his release from jail and was admitted to the bar.
He practiced in the James River settlement of Howardsville
in Albermarle County. He married Pauline Clark of Franklin,
Kentucky on 30 December 1857. The then United States
Senator Andrew Johnson, a friend of her family, was among
the guests at the wedding. Mosby then moved to Bristol, Virginia and hung up his shingle. He was among Bristol's first
lawyers.

The first child of John and Pauline, a daughter, arrived on
10 May 1859. They were happy, but in the midst of their
happiness, national sentiment about the slavery question was
reaching crisis proportions. States rights and slavery and the

invasion expected from the North made up the conversation. Mosby kept his political views to himself, but he spoke up as a strong supporter of the Douglas ticket in the election of 1860. He argued against Southern secession. This was the first evidence that he would take an independent and unpopular position in politics. One of his biographers said that his habit was "to lean against the wind."

In 1861, while attending court in Abingdon, the county seat, Mosby learned from his University of Virginia classmate William Blackford (later of Jeb Stuart's Cavalry and an author in his own right on Stuart), that Blackford and others were trying to raise a cavalry unit and wanted Mosby to join. Thinking that not to join would indicate a lack of patriotism, and after discussing it with Pauline, he decided to join.

At the first meeting of the newly formed militia company, Mosby arrived on a borrowed horse. It was an inauspicious beginning for a young man who envisaged serving in the cavalry and who was to become a legend in the cavalry.

The commander of the new military company was William E. Jones, known in Civil War history as "Grumble" Jones, an experienced soldier who had graduated with honors from West Point. He had resigned from the Army in 1857, but when the bugle blew over the South, "Grumble" Jones reported for duty. Jones had a profound influence on Mosby. The company took the name "Washington's Mounted Rifles" after Washington County, where the troopers resided. Mosby was granted time off from the first days of intensive training to wind down his law business and to get a horse from his father's farm. He finally made his last court appearance at Blountsville, Tennessee.

Meanwhile, a baby son had arrived, named Beverly Clark Mosby for his grandfather.

Mosby took enthusiastically to his new occupation as a soldier. General Robert E. Lee was made commander of the military and naval forces in Virginia, and "Grumble" Jones was commissioned a major in the Virginia Volunteers, but remained commander of the Washington Mounted Rifles for a time. A number of Virginia companies were mustered into service along with the Washington Rifles. They were ordered to Richmond and continued to train there. Mosby saw a story in the newspaper that a corps of mounted guerilla rangers were being created to serve in General Wise's brigade, and the article stated that the movement had been sanctioned by President Jefferson Davis. It reminded Mosby of Francis Marion of Revolutionary War fame.

One of his friends offered to get Mosby a commission, but Mosby declined on the ground that he had no previous military training and that it would be much better for him to continue to serve as a private under such an able commander as "Grumble" Jones.

Stuart's Brigade, of which the Rifles were a part, was involved in only skirmishes during the winter months of 1861–1862. Meanwhile, Mosby was promoted to first lieutenant and adjutant. Mosby had a six-day furlough in January of 1862 on the strength of a recommendation from "Grumble" Jones that Mosby left home as a lawyer in good practice and was always ready for the most active and dangerous duty, rendering brilliant service.

In March, Mosby wrote home that he intended to stay in the foremost ranks, "where life is lost or freedom won." He said he wanted to see in the Southern women some of the Spartan heroism displayed by the Spartan mother who said to her son when she buckled on his armor, "Return with your shield or return upon it."

Word came to Stuart that Johnson wanted to know if McClellan's army was trailing him or whether his movements were just a feint, whereupon Mosby said, "Give me a guide, and I'll find out for you." By the next morning, Mosby, muddy and wet, reported that the enemy was feinting, and Stuart sent "Grumble" Jones to disperse the isolated column which Mosby found. For this scouting, Mosby gained his first mention in Confederate records, when he was recommended for promotion because of his scouting service that night.

At this point, the Confederate Congress allowed the soldiers to vote on who should be their commanding officers. In Stuart's Brigade, Fitzhugh Lee won out over "Grumble" Jones, and Mosby promptly resigned his commission. He did not want to serve under Fitzhugh Lee, a person he had never liked. Stuart assured Mosby that he would get his commission back in some other way, and Stuart put him on his staff as a courier.

Just preceding the Seven Days Campaign in 1862, Robert E. Lee, who had replaced the wounded General Johnson, directed Stuart to get more exact information about the enemy's position. Stuart, in turn, sent Mosby, who came back with the valuable information that the cavalry could completely circle McClellan's army on a route that Mosby had picked out. This was done immediately by a force of 1,200 cavalrymen, which created the impression that Lee was sending support to Jackson in the valley of Virginia when the exact opposite was happening. Jackson was on the way to help Lee. The cavalrymen ended up riding more than 100 miles, completely around McClellan's army, capturing many prisoners, horses, and mules while losing only one soldier themselves. Mosby rode ahead the entire way as a guide. This highly publicized ride stirred the Southern cause and allowed Lee to speed his plans for the Seven Days Campaign, which was based on the information supplied from that ride.

This led to another general order commending Mosby and others, and within a week, he was sent to the office of Secretary of War Randolph with a note signed by Stuart:

Permit me to present to you John S. Mosby, who for months past has rendered time and again services of the most important and valuable nature, exposing himself regardless of danger, and, in my estimation, fairly won promotion.

I am anxious that he should get the captain of sharp-shooters in my brigade, but the muster rolls have not yet been sent in. I commend him to your notice.

Quiet followed the Seven Days Campaign, and nothing was heard from Secretary of War Randolph. General John Pope, in taking command of the Federal forces in the valley and around Washington, announced his policy of allowing lines of retreat to take care of themselves, saying "Let us look before us and not behind." Mosby immediately saw the opportunity in falling upon the unguarded Union rear. Stuart listened to Mosby's arguments for a second command, but said he did not have the men to spare. He suggested that Jackson might supply Mosby's needs.

In July 1862, Mosby set out to see Jackson, carrying a letter from Stuart, and a newly published copy of Napoleon's *Maxims of War*, which Stuart wanted Jackson to read. En route, Mosby was captured and sent to the old Capital Prison in Washington. Ten days later, to be exchanged, he and other prisoners were loaded on a ship and sent down the Potomac to Fort Monroe and thence up the James River to the point of exchange. The ever-vigilant Mosby scouted en route. He saw several transports loaded with troops and learned that they were part of Burnside's army, then in North Carolina. He surmised that they were going either to support McClellan at Harrison's Landing or to reinforce Pope in his advance on Richmond from Fredericksburg.

As soon as he could get to Richmond, he went to General Lee's headquarters, where he had trouble getting in, being described as an unkempt figure with stooped shoulders. He said he had important news for General Lee. He was denied entrance, but he protested so loudly that a staff officer came out, heard his plea, and admitted him. He reported that General Burnside's troops were on the way to Aquina Creek to reinforce Pope, saying, "I've just come from Hampton Roads, where I saw them." He also told General Lee that he was one of the men mentioned in his general order in connection with General Stuart's ride around McClellan, thinking that Lee might attach more weight to his information given that knowledge. Lee replied that he did remember that event and gave an order for the information to be sent to Jackson's headquarters immediately.

Following his interchange, Mosby returned to duty with Stuart. He participated in the Second Battle of Manassas in August, Antietam in September, Stuart's raid into Chambersburg, Pennsylvania in October, and the Battle of Fredericksburg, Virginia in December. Then, at this point, Mosby, still hoping for a command, was given a detail of men by Stuart and permission to remain behind when Stuart's cavalry left for winter quarters west of Fredericksburg. This meant that he was staying behind in Loudoun County near Alday, to conduct guerilla forays during the winter months.

As Virgil Carrington Jones wrote in *Ranger Mosby*, "The strange little band that struck across Fairfax County in early January, '63, was Destiny's evidence the Devil had thrown loaded dice against part of the Yankee Army."

Mosby did not look much like a warrior. One of his rangers who first glimpsed Mosby in the spring of 1863 when he became a recruit, said that he could scarcely believe that the slight figure before him could be that of the man who had won such military fame for his daring. Another one of his men, John Munson, described him as "fair of complexion, slight, but wiry, with a military belt on from which hung two Colt Army pistols." Munson could not believe the quiet demeanor of Mosby and his lack of swagger. He stood 5' 7-8" and weighed about 125 pounds, and he had a slight stoop in his posture, which made him seem even shorter. Mosby said of himself that he was the frailest and most delicate man in the company when he enlisted in 1861. By 1863, his body had been toughened, and there were few, if any, who could match his endurance. One of his men described him as "hatchet-faced" and with a "hawk-like nose." One thing different about him was his eyes. None who served with him would ever forget his blue, luminous, piercing eyes, which had a marked effect on his men.

One of his other men said that he always spoke in a quiet voice, that he was reserved, but there was no mistaking the meaning of his words. Mosby cared neither for sentiment nor for pretense. There was a hard realism to him. At the same time, he possessed a "rich vein of humor" and contributed to the camaraderie and laughter around the campfire or at a dinner.

One of Jeb Stuart's staff said that Mosby had an active, daring, and penetrating mind and that he was a deep thinker. His raids were planned and calculated. Mosby was also a restless man, rarely sitting still for ten minutes. He had untiring energy and would spend hours in the saddle, scouting Union lines and gathering information from civilians. It was said that he studied, prepared, and then struck. Stuart's staff member said that Mosby's tirelessness, his dauntlessness, his daring, and his intellect made him a formidable opponent.

Mosby chose a mission which would unleash a maelstrom in Northern Virginia, his battleground. His independent command, which began with a nine-man detail, was the beginning of twenty-eight months of raids, ambushes, and attacks against Union forces in the region, which stretched from the outskirts of Washington across the Blue Ridge Mountains into the Shenandoah Valley and beyond the Potomac River into Maryland. The war would be decided in this region. The great battles before and after Gettysburg took place there.

The terrain in this part of Virginia was conducive to guerilla warfare. There were hundreds of square miles of forests and mountains and fertile farmlands. A single sentry on horseback stationed on a knoll could scan miles of territory for enemy units. There was a good network of lanes and obscure trails for movement, many places of refuge, and a network of informants in small towns and homes of planters and yeoman farmers.

As Mosby stated, his purpose was to "weaken the armies invading Virginia by harassing their rear."[3] Mosby and his men rode from Fauquier and Loudoun Counties, striking in the dark of night or the glare of day, at unexpected places, in good weather and bad. It was warfare predicated upon speed, mobility, and surprise attacks—the tactics of thrust before parry. However, it generated bitterness between antagonists, and even the cloak of romance that surrounds guerilla activity could not conceal the killing and the maiming it left behind. As 1862 slipped into 1863, Americans of the North and South began to see the sacrifice and cost of war.

Mosby conducted only one small operation with his nine-man detail, and this was on 10 January 1863. He then reported to Stuart and requested a fifteen-man detail, saying that he could make the Federal commander in Fairfax County contract his lines. He was given the extra men to operate within enemy lines and to provide Stuart with reconnaissance reports.

These fifteen men, members of the First Virginia Cavalry, were detached from Brigadier General Fitzhugh Lee's com-

---

[3]As in William A. Tidwell, *Confederate Covert Action in the American Civil War* (Kent OH: Kent State University Press, 1995) 165.

mand. It was believed that they were handpicked by Mosby. By this time, Mosby was a captain. The fifteen included twenty-one-year-old Fountain Beattie, later a pallbearer at Mosby's funeral, and others who became great soldiers in their own right. This was the beginning of the 43rd Battalion. Mosby's activities became so infuriating to the Union Army as to cause threats of burning of towns, and at one point several citizens of Middleburg petitioned Mosby to discontinue his operations.

The "Rangers," as members of Mosby's command came to be called, had more than their share of victories and some defeats. The daring capture of General Stoughton from his bed, the fights at Miskel's Farm, Second Dranesville, Mt. Zion Church, the Berryville Wagon Raid, and many others are chronicled in the official records of the war.

Mosby apparently had no trouble recruiting for his battalion. Men were attracted by the adventure and the spoils, which Confederate law and Mosby permitted the men to keep. Each person had to provide his own horse, but that seemed to have been no problem given the spoils of the raids.

Many of the recruits became leaders and reliable soldiers. One of these recruits, "Big Yankee" Ames, was a member of the 5th New York Cavalry. He walked to Fauquier County, near Middleburg, and found Mosby. He wanted to join Mosby and leave the Union because of President Lincoln's Emancipation Proclamation. Ames and a colleague from the 5th New York Cavalry actually went back to their unit and stole two horses and brought five extra horses out of the stables. Ames was later killed, and Mosby said of him that he had never had a more faithful follower.

Service in the 43rd Battalion carried a price. According to Jeffrey Wert, in his *Mosby's Rangers*, Ranger casualties amounted to between thirty-five to forty percent of the command. The author thought that at least eighty-five identified members of the command were killed, mortally wounded or executed. He stated that 477 Rangers were captured by the Federals during the command's existence, but many of these were exchanged and returned to the Battalion.

The Rangers inflicted great cost on the Federal forces and supplied invaluable intelligence to Robert E. Lee and to Jeb Stuart. At times, they severed Union lines of communication and supply. All of these were important accomplishments, but Professor Wert summed it up by saying that in the end, although Mosby and the Rangers prevailed in their war of wits, the 43rd Battalion neither prolonged the war for several months nor did they keep thousands of Union troops away from the front, as had been hoped.

War is always cruel, but hardly anything exceeds the conduct of General George Custer in executing six Rangers at Front Royal, Virginia in 1864. He was following Grant's order to hang without trial Mosby's men if caught. One was a seventeen-year-old boy from Front Royal, while his mother screamed to save his life. One of the six to be executed was William Thomas Overby of Georgia. Defiant, erect, he refused to tell where Mosby was, saying as had the others, "We cannot tell you that." As his last words, Overby said, "Mosby'll hang ten of you for every one of us." Custer witnessed the executions.

Mosby was wounded at the time and out of action, but with Lee's permission, he notified the Union Commander, General Sheridan, that he considered what Custer had done to be uncivilized and outside the rules of war, and that it would be necessary for him to repay by executing an equal number of Federal soldiers of Custer's command. This was done by selecting six by lot from twenty-seven prisoners, which six included a drummer boy. Mosby had little stomach for what he was doing and ordered the drummer boy released and a substitute chosen. Two of the group escaped, and no effort was made to recapture them. This whole chapter was a sad commentary on the war, but there is no record of other executions by either side.

After Lee surrendered at Appomattox, the Northern commanders, including General Hancock, made every effort to get Mosby to surrender his command. Several meetings were held with the Federals, all very civil, but Mosby decided instead to call his Rangers together for one last time. Much later, at the reunion of his battalion in 1895, Mosby said: "Life cannot afford a more bitter cup than the one I drained when we parted at Salem, nor any higher reward of ambition than that I received as commander of the 43rd Virginia Battalion of Cavalry."[4]

On 21 April 1865, a few days after Appomattox, Mosby disbanded the 43rd Battalion rather than to surrender it. Within the next few days, most of the men received individual paroles.

Mosby did not surrender and, indeed, had been told that he would not be given parole if he did surrender. He was never captured but finally sought parole after being assured that he would receive it. Thus came the end of his career as a soldier on 13 June 1865. The war was lost. Many of his Rangers had been killed, and his heroes Generals Stuart and "Grumble" Jones had both gone to their reward in battles a few months earlier.

The men of the 43rd returned to civilian life and became farmers, carpenters, livestock breeders, teachers, merchants, and businessmen. Some, like their commander, were lawyers. Others practiced medicine. Some were policemen, and quite a number became ministers. A few became U.S. marshals or

---

[4]*The Memoirs of Colonel John S. Mosby*, ed. Charles Wells (Boston: Little, Brown, 1917) xviii.

postmasters. A striking number found employment with the Federal government, an irony of sorts.

Joseph Bryan became a noted publisher, and his descendants today own the Richmond, Virginia newspapers. Walter Gosden, one of the Rangers, fathered a son, Freeman Gosden, who entered show business as "Amos" of "Amos and Andy."

Another of the Rangers, Charles McDonough, never surrendered. He refused parole and evaded Union patrols until he was finally hunted down in June 1865. Surrounded by Federal soldiers, he emptied his pistol except for one round and, placing the muzzle in his mouth, squeezed the trigger. The conflict had taken its last Ranger.

Mosby planned to move to Warrenton, Virginia and open a law office, but in August, he was arrested by the forces of occupation in Alexandria when a near riot occurred as crowds began following Mosby. He was in jail for two days.

Later that month, Mosby was reported to be in Richmond at the grave of Stuart, and he was described as a solitary man who plucked a wildflower, dropping it on the gravestone.

His troubles were not over. He opened his law office in Warrenton and was doing well in his practice when he was arrested by the Federal provost marshal while in Leesburg on business, apparently only for being outside Warrenton. Pauline went directly to President Johnson to have her husband released. She was treated in a cold manner, although Johnson was a friend of her family and had attended her wedding. She was not to be put off and turned to General Grant, where she was graciously received. Grant ordered Mosby's release and wrote out a parole for Mosby in his own hand. Thus ended Mosby's problem with the Federals and the occupation.

Grant was elected president in 1868, and during Grant's first term, Mosby stayed out of national politics, carried on his law practice, and generally readjusted to civilian and family life. Although Pauline met General Grant when getting the parole, Mosby never actually met Grant until shortly before Grant ran for reelection in 1871. Mosby thought it was in the interest of the South to support Grant rather than Horace Greely, the candidate of the Democrats. This caused great resentment against Mosby in Virginia, even though Grant ended up carrying Virginia in the election. Shortly thereafter, Grant personally thanked Mosby for his help.

Mosby continued his law practice and unsuccessfully ran for Congress. Pauline died in 1876, after giving birth to their eighth child. That same year, Grant asked his successor, President Hayes, to give Mosby an appointment. The resentment against Mosby for supporting Grant had not abated, and it had bothered President Grant. Mosby was appointed consul to Hong Kong, where he remained for seven years. His consulship ended with the election of President Cleveland.

He then, again through the auspices of General Grant, accepted a position as counsel with the Southern Pacific Railroad. This required him to live in San Francisco, but he made many trips to Virginia. The railroad was reorganized, and he lost that job after nearly twenty years.

President McKinley gave him a special appointment as a land agent in the General Land Office of the Federal government. He worked there for three years until Teddy Roosevelt, at the urging of Virginia friends, gave him a job as an assistant attorney general at the Department of Justice, where he worked until 1910. He then wrote and lectured until his death in 1916 at the age of 83.

Throughout his postwar years, Mosby visited with his Ranger friends, some of whom outlived him. One notable friend was Dr. Aristides Monterio, a University of Virginia classmate, who joined the 43rd Battalion as its surgeon in 1864 and remained Mosby's close friend over the years.

Another was Fountain Beattie, one of the great Ranger heroes.

Perhaps the highlight of Mosby's last years was when a delegation from the University of Virginia brought him a token of appreciation, considering that the University had expelled him in 1853. It consisted of a medallion on which were words to express the affection and esteem of his friends and admirers at the University. The inscription said, in part:

> Endowed with the gift of friendship, which won for you the confidence of both Lee and Grant, you have proven yourself a man of war, a man of letters, and a man of affairs worthy of the best traditions of your University and your State, to both of which you have been a loyal son.

Mosby lived until 1916, but nothing in his postwar career, as is the case with many warriors, could rise to the level of his war career. He attended an occasional Ranger reunion, and he wrote copiously in defense of Stuart's delay in reaching Gettysburg. Stuart's delay deprived General Lee of knowledge of the Federal troop movement, allowing the Federal forces to take the high ground and win the battle. Mosby was disputing the indisputable, still facing against the wind. His last year was spent in writing his own memoirs, which were published the year after his death.[5]

Mosby died in Washington, and a train carried his remains to Warrenton. He was buried beside Pauline and his deceased children. Down a slope not far away, Professor Wert notes, was the grave of Richard Montjoy, another one of his Ranger heroes who had been killed in the war. Mosby had written for Montjoy's tomb in a general order:

---

[5] *The Memoirs of Colonel John S. Mosby*, ed. Charles Wells Russell (Boston: Little, Brown, and Co., 1917). The full text, including illustrations, is posted online: <http://docsouth.unc.edu/fpn/mosby/mosby.html>.

[H]is death was a costly sacrifice to Victory. He died too early for liberty and his country's cause, but not too early for his own fame.

Virgil Carrington Jones, the author of *Ranger Mosby*, said of Mosby's own burial:

So John Singleton Mosby, lawyer, soldier, patriot, author, was buried in appropriate company [near a shaft marking the mound under which lay the bodies of 500 soldiers] on the brow of a hill at Warrenton, overlooking the green fields through which had romped his phantom legion. They buried him two days after he died, but 52 years too late to bring him the glory he deserved.

General Grant wrote in his own memoirs:

Since the close of the war, I have come to know Colonel Mosby personally and somewhat intimately. He is a different man entirely from what I had supposed. . . .

He is able and thoroughly honest and truthful. There were but probably few men in the South who could have commanded successfully a separate detachment, in the rear of an opposing army and so near the border of hostilities, as long as he did without losing his entire command.

Perhaps Mosby would have been better served had he been killed in combat. He might have achieved immortality and stood with Jackson, Stuart, the Gallant Pelham, "Grumble" Jones, and the long list of others who died in the Southern Cause and were spared defeat. Their crowning glory was in their death. Like Mosby's words on Montjoy's tomb, they died too early for liberty, but not for their own fame.

Chapter 9

The Peace Conference at Hampton Roads

A Missed Opportunity [1]

I.

Historically, racial conflict has been America's most abiding problem. In the first 150 years of the Republic, slavery was replaced by government-imposed segregation, and the conflict remained. The solution was finally compelled by sweeping changes arising out the technological revolution of the last fifty years and the thrust of rising expectations.

The historical perspective of the race problem during the first 150 years includes three distinct failures in the face of magnificent opportunities presented for resolution.

The first failure was that of the Founding Fathers at the Constitutional Convention. The next was administered by the Supreme Court in the *Dred Scott* decision. The third was the Hampton Roads Peace Conference of 1865. Though little more than a footnote to history, the Hampton Roads Conference was a lost opportunity of calamitous proportions. In a causal sense, it may have been the most significant of the failures. Success rather than failure at Hampton Roads might have prevented the excesses of Reconstruction and the subsequent breakdown in race relations which lasted for almost 100 years.

---

[1]Editor's note. Judge Bell became a member of The Ten in 1974, and he presented this paper to the group on 26 September of that year.

Slavery had come to the American Colonies in 1619 when the master of a Dutch man-of-war sold twenty slaves to the Virginia colonists at Jamestown.

By 1787, at the time of the Constitutional Convention, there were slaves in every state except Massachusetts, where slavery had recently been abolished by court decision. There were a total of 677,681 slaves, 59,527 free persons of color, and 3,171,006 whites in the states at the time of the Convention.

Slavery was the subject of some discussion at the Constitutional Convention, but it was a controversial issue and the Founding Fathers postponed its resolution. Their prime interest was in forming a Union. They preserved the right of each state to import slaves prior to the year 1808. They also preserved the property rights of slaveowners by having the states pledge to deliver up any slave who might have escaped and who was found within their respective territories. There was no substantial effort at the Convention to abolish the institution of slavery; it was in fact condoned.

The deep feeling of many Americans against slavery was manifested almost immediately. Statutes were enacted to curtail the importation of slaves by restricting the use of property for that purpose, notwithstanding the leeway given in the Constitution prior to the year 1808. Although drastic statutes were passed after 1808 to prohibit importation, enforcement of the statutes was halfhearted. One author has said that the main effort to restrict slavery was made by the British in patrolling the west coast of Africa.

Eli Whitney invented the cotton gin in 1792. Cotton became king in the South and this, in turn, led to an increased demand for slave labor. The trend for a few years had been to free slaves, and by 1810 there were almost 200,000 "free persons of color" in the states. Although this trend receded, the number had increased to almost 500,000 by 1860.

Meanwhile, the number of slaves had increased to 4,000,000 and the number of whites to 31,000,000. In Georgia alone, there were 462,000 slaves, more than half as many as the total of all slaves in America in 1787.

The national debate over slavery resulted in the Missouri Compromise of 1820, the first effort by Congress to preclude slavery. The purpose of Congress was to contain slavery until abolished in the original slave states, and to prevent its spread to most of the newly acquired Louisiana Territory. Slavery was being gradually eliminated in the original states. The states as sovereign governments, acting in the Congress of 1787, which was organized under Articles of Confederation and preceded the Constitution, had precluded slavery in the Northwest Territory (later the states of Ohio, Indiana, Illinois, Michigan, and Wisconsin).

Under the Missouri Compromise, Missouri was admitted as a slaveholding state, but slavery was prohibited in the territories of the United States north of Missouri's southern boundary and latitude 36°30'. Maine, which had just detached itself from Massachusetts, was admitted to the Union, making twelve free and twelve slave states.

This compromise lasted for thirty-six years until it was destroyed by the Supreme Court in 1856 in the *Dred Scott* decision. Lincoln was later to argue that a nation could not exist half slave and half free, but this was the shape of the nation after *Dred Scott.*

The Supreme Court, by denying national citizenship to persons of African descent, effectively blocked any hope of the slavery question being resolved by the states alone. It was the moment in history when the court could have ameliorated slavery as a great national issue. The court could have followed the lead of those slave states which held that once taken into a free state or territory by his or her master, a slave was free for all purposes. Once free, even under the Articles of Confederation, the former slave became a national citizen. But the court turned its back to the problem in a singular act of regression.

The issue in *Dred Scott* was whether slaves taken into the nonslave states and into free territory became free by virtue of the laws of those states or, in the case of the slave-free territory, the federal law. Dred Scott and his wife and children sued in Missouri in the federal court in an effort to obtain their freedom from John Sandford, a resident of New York. They had been sold to John Sandford by the widow of Dr. John Emerson, an Army doctor. (Sandford was antislavery, and the lawsuit may have been contrived.)

They claimed their freedom by virtue of having been taken to Illinois and also into the Minnesota territory north of 36°30′ latitude. Indeed, one of the two children had been born in the free territory.

The Supreme Court, in a 5-2 decision, reached two conclusions in the case. One, persons of African descent were not entitled to sue as citizens in the courts of the United States, being regarded legally as mere property or chattels. No state was empowered to make one of the black race a citizen of the United States or to endow such a person with the rights of citizenship in the other states of the Union without their consent. The descendants of Africans who were imported into this country and sold as slaves, even when emancipated, or who were born of free parents, were not citizens as that term was used in the Constitution of the United States.

Second, and this holding was unnecessary to the decision, the words of the Constitution should be given the meaning they were intended to bear when the Constitution was framed and adopted. The right of property in slaves was distinctly and expressly affirmed in the Constitution. The Missouri Compromise, prohibiting the holding and owning of slaves in parts of the Louisiana Territory, was not warranted by the

Constitution and was therefore void. Dred Scott and his family remained the property of the defendant John Sandford.

The two dissenting justices were of a different view. First, free persons, although descended from Africans held in slavery, were citizens of the United States under the Articles of Confederation and consequently were national citizens at the time of the adoption of the Constitution of the United States. The dissenters pointed out that at the time of the ratification of the Articles of Confederation, all free native-born inhabitants of New Hampshire, Massachusetts, New York, New Jersey, and North Carolina, though descended from African slaves, were citizens of those states and were allowed to vote. Indeed, the Articles of Confederation provided:

> Article IV. The better to secure and perpetuate mutual friendship and intercourse among the people of the different States of this Union, the free inhabitants of each of these States, paupers, vagabonds, and fugitives from justice excepted, shall be entitled to all privileges and immunities of free citizens in the several States. . . . [2]

It followed, they said, that every free person who was a citizen of a state by force of its constitution or laws was also a citizen of the United States. This position, well founded in law and logic, would have extended national citizenship and constitutional protection to any person of African descent who was freeborn or who had been manumitted by the master or by the fact of being taken into a nonslavery jurisdiction if permitted by state law.

It was the law in several of the slave states at the time, including Kentucky, Louisiana, Maryland, Mississippi, and Virginia, that the taking of a slave into a nonslave state or

---

[2]See "U.S. Constitution online. The Articles of Confederation," at <http://www.usconstitution.net/articles.html>.

territory freed the slave, *ipso facto*. This had been the law in Missouri until Dred Scott lost his case in the courts of that state prior to bringing his federal suit.

The Supreme Court, however, as the final enunciator of the law of the land, obliterated any possibility of a descendant of an African slave ever being an American citizen under any condition regardless of what the states might do. Any gradual movement toward abolition (except on a state basis) and toward national citizenship for blacks was truncated.

The court ignored the maxim that public opinion has a place in the institution of justice. As Tocqueville said of the Supreme Court and federal judges after touring America in 1831:

> Their [federal judges'] power is enormous, but it is the power of public opinion. They are all-powerful so long as the people consent to obey the law; they can do nothing when they scorn it. . . .

> The federal judges, therefore, must not only be good citizens and men of education and integrity, qualities necessary for all magistrates, but must also be statesmen; they must know how to understand the spirit of the age, to confront those obstacles that can be overcome, and steer out of the current when the tide threatens to carry them away, and with them the sovereignty of the Union and obedience to its laws.[3]

History now records that the *Dred Scott* case was caught up in the political currents of the day. Indeed, three of the justices secretly advised President-Elect Buchanan of the two dissenters' proposal to uphold the Missouri Compromise and

---

[3]Alexis de Tocqueville, *The Republic of the United States of America, and Its Political Institutions, Review and Examined* (half-title: *Democracy in America*), two volumes in one (New York: A. S. Barnes, 1851) vol. 1, chap. 8, "The Federal Constitution."

sought his help in getting votes on the court for a contrary position. Although the issue was not before the court, the Missouri Compromise was invalidated. President Buchanan, based on his inside information, was able to say in his inaugural address, two days before the opinion was issued, that the slavery issue should be left to the Supreme Court where it was then pending and would be decided.

The safety valve having thus been closed, the Civil War began in five years. Its cost in men and treasure was staggering. For example, one out of every six Georgians served in the Confederate forces. One out of every four who served was lost. Three-fourths of all property in the Confederate states, including all currency and slave property, was lost. The southern region of the nation was left in poverty or near poverty for fifty years or more. One civilization ended and another began. A principal impediment to future race relations was that the heritage of the South became the heritage of the "lost cause," nurtured in poverty and the experiences of Reconstruction.

The great aim of the Southern white was to return as nearly as possible to the status quo ante. The Hayes-Tilden political accommodation eventually ended Reconstruction and a near status quo ante in the form of state-imposed segregation and denial of the franchise to the blacks was not long in coming.

This status quo was not significantly altered until the 1960s, when the right to the franchise was finally restored to blacks in the South, along with the elimination of segregation in public institutions and facilities, and of discrimination in some other areas of life.

II.

Whether the post-Civil War racial problems might have been avoided depends in large measure on how the Civil War ended and on the events immediately following the Civil War. There was one fleeting period in early 1865 when a spirit of reconciliation in ending the war and rebuilding the country hung in the balance.

This moment came in the form of a conference between President Lincoln and Alexander Stephens, the Confederacy's vice president, at Hampton Roads, Virginia in February 1865. Although the effort proved futile, the event is worth recalling as we move through the third century of our Republic. The lesson to be gained from the failure of the conference may tend to sustain and even rekindle that spirit of compromise and compassion that is so necessary in a republic made up of diverse peoples of many customs.

The Hampton Roads Peace Conference was prompted by Horace Greeley, the editor of the *New York Tribune*. The war was not going well for the South, and on 14 January 1865, Francis P. Blair, Sr., a Washington journalist and political figure, was seen in Richmond. It was later learned through the press that he had dined with President and Mrs. Davis. This gave rise to much speculation in the North and the South regarding the "Blair Mission" to Richmond. One of Blair's sons was in President Lincoln's cabinet and another was a corps commander in Sherman's army, while Blair himself was a counselor to Lincoln, as he had been to President Jackson.

Greeley had the idea that President Lincoln had shown a spirit of conciliation in his public statements. He felt that it was time to undertake open peace negotiations with the Confederates, at least to the point of putting the Confederates in the position of refusing peace.

Greeley suggested that Blair undertake the effort toward peace. It developed that Blair had written President Lincoln several months earlier in this regard. Blair went to Lincoln in mid-December 1864, but Lincoln deferred the matter, saying, "Come to me after Savannah falls."

A few days later General Sherman presented Savannah to President Lincoln as a Christmas present. Three days later, Lincoln wrote one sentence on a card: "Allow the bearer, F. P. Blair, Sr. to pass our lines, go South, and return."

Blair departed for General Grant's headquarters at City Point on the James River and from there addressed a note to his friend, Jefferson Davis, a former secretary of war and United States senator, advising that he wished to discuss a confidential matter with him. Davis's reply miscarried, and Blair, disappointed, returned to Washington.

The Davis reply finally reached Blair, who returned to Grant's headquarters on the James River and from there went to Richmond. Blair dined with Davis at the Confederate White House and visited with friends of other days. Blair assured Davis that he did not speak for President Lincoln, but inquired whether Davis was tied to any European power that might stop him from doing what he might want to in connection with the government of the United States. Davis replied that he was tied in no way.

Blair then produced a paper, prepared by him, which contained the proposition that the Confederate states come back into the Union on the basis of taking an oath of allegiance to the Union and ending slavery. The fighting would be stopped on an understanding that Davis head up combined armies to enforce the Monroe Doctrine against the French establishment in Mexico. The idea was to end the Civil War by an agreement to invade Mexico, drive Maxmillian from his throne there, and add Mexico to the United States.

Blair was given a letter by Davis which authorized him to repeat the substance of their conversation to President Lincoln, and which stated that he was willing to enter into negotiations for the restoration of peace between "the two countries." In his written report to President Lincoln, Blair stated that Davis looked with some favor on the general outline and would be willing to send conferees to Mr. Lincoln.

Blair then told Lincoln of his Mexican offer to Davis. This was news to President Lincoln, and he stated that he had not the slightest interest in it but was impressed by Blair's report that the morale of the Confederate leaders was low. He was also impressed by the letter from Davis and thereupon addressed Davis, by way of Blair, as follows.

Washington, January 18, 1865

F. P. Blair, Esq.

Sir:

You having shown me Mr. Davis's letter to you of the 12th instant, you may say to him that I have constantly been, am now, and shall continue to be ready to receive any agent whom he, or any other influential person now resisting the national authority, may informally send to me, with the view of securing peace to the people of our one common country.

Yours, etc.,
    A. Lincoln

While Davis had referred to "the two countries," Lincoln's letter ended with the phrase "our one common country." This was a vital distinction. Lincoln also referred to Davis as *Mr.* Davis rather than as *President* Davis.

Blair returned to Richmond with the letter and while there attempted to excuse the Mexican offer. Davis seemed to accept that the offer was Blair's and not Lincoln's.

Blair returned to Washington, and Davis moved to send commissioners to meet with Lincoln. He sent for Vice President Stephens to meet him in conference and also advised his cabinet that he proposed sending commissioners to meet Lincoln for the purpose of negotiating peace.

Stephens argued that Davis should meet directly with Lincoln. Davis demurred, and Stephens suggested the names of three commissioners. He found himself in agreement with Davis as to one of the names, John A. Campbell, formerly an associate justice of the Supreme Court of the United States who resigned from the court at the beginning of the Civil War. Stephens also suggested General Henry L. Benning, formerly a justice of the Supreme Court of Georgia and then commanding a brigade near City Point, and Thomas F. Flournoy, a distinguished Virginian who was well known personally to Mr. Lincoln. Davis decided instead to appoint his friend, Confederate Senator R. M. T. Hunter, formerly a United States Senator, and Stephens himself.

Davis then armed the three commissioners with the letter from Mr. Lincoln, and also a letter instructing them to proceed to Washington City for an informal conference with Mr. Lincoln upon the issues involved in the existing war, and for the purpose of securing peace "to the two countries." His letter was dated 28 January 1865.

Excitement over the pending prospects mounted in the North and South. The Richmond press accused Davis of consorting with the enemy and suggested that he take up abode in the North. Henry Ward Beecher complained directly to Lincoln of his fear that out of a desire for peace the South would be given the advantage.

The Confederate commissioners, seeking passage to Washington, were received at City Point by General Grant on the evening of 29 January. Upon being advised of their presence by Grant, Lincoln dispatched Major Eckert from

Washington with written directions to Grant to afford the commissioners safe conduct if they were ready to talk peace on the basis of his note of 18 January for "our one common country." Before Eckert arrived, General Grant had visited with the commissioners and later wrote that he had been a particular admirer of Mr. Stephens.

Stephens wrote of Grant that he afforded them comfortable quarters on board one of his dispatch boats. He was much impressed with Grant as a person. He stated that Grant made it evident to Stephens that he was anxious for the proposed peace conference to take place.

During his latter life, Stephens published a letter which he received from General Grant in answer to his request to cross the federal lines en route to Washington. General Grant acknowledged the request and replied that he was instructing the commanding officer of his forces near Petersburg to allow Stephens and his group to cross and he hoped to have a reply from Washington by the time they reached City Point. Grant also said that in the event their request to proceed to Washington was denied, "I promise you a safe and immediate return within your own lines."

Lincoln, in the meantime, had decided not to meet with the commissioners personally, but to send Secretary of State Seward to meet them at Fort Monroe. He gave Seward written instructions to make it known to the commissioners that there were three indispensable elements to peace: the restoration of the national authority throughout all of their states, the end of slavery, and no cessation of hostilities short of an end of the war and a disbanding of forces hostile to the national government. Lincoln also advised Grant not to delay any military moves or plans pending the conference.

Major Eckert finally arrived with the out-of-date instructions that the conference could be held only if the commissioners would state in writing that they were ready to talk peace on the basis of President Lincoln's note of 18 January for "our one common country." After some hours of discussion, the commissioners refused to comply, and they were told they could not proceed.

Grant became upset over the impasse and took matters into his own hands. He sent Secretary of War Stanton a long telegram urging that the intentions of the commissioners were good and their desire sincere to restore peace and union. He stated that he regretted that Mr. Lincoln could not at least have an interview with Stephens and Hunter.

Lincoln walked over to the War Office the next morning, read Major Eckert's report, and was framing a telegram to call Seward back from Fort Monroe when Grant's telegram was put in his hands. He later wrote that the telegram "changed my purpose" and he at once wired Grant: "Say to the gentlemen I will meet them personally at Fortress Monroe as soon as I can get there."

Lincoln cancelled his appointments and left for Fort Monroe on the morning of the 2nd of February. He did not advise his cabinet that he was leaving, or of his purpose.

He boarded a naval vessel which sailed down the Potomac, into Chesapeake Bay, and on to Hampton Roads and docked alongside Fort Monroe. (Hampton Roads is a channel near Newport News, Portsmouth, and Norfolk through which waters of the James, Nansemond, and Elizabeth Rivers flow into the Chesapeake Bay.)

Stephens had been close to Lincoln when they served as Whig members of the House of Representatives in the 1840s. They had opposed the Mexican War and were among those who started the Taylor-for-President movement.

Lincoln was once so moved by a Stephens speech on the grandeur and misery of war, at the time of the Mexican War, that he wrote to his law partner:

Mr. Stephens, of Georgia, a little, slim, pale-faced consumptive man . . . has just concluded the very best speech of an hour's length that I ever heard. My own withered dry eyes are full of tears yet.[4]

Lincoln later wrote that on arrival he found Secretary Seward and Major Eckert on a steamer anchored off Fort Monroe in Hampton Roads and learned that the Confederate commissioners were on another nearby steamer and that Seward had not yet seen them.

On the morning of 3 February, the commissioners came aboard Lincoln's steamer for the meeting. Seward advised that no notes would be taken, but there is little difference among the recollections of the five men present as to what occurred.

All present remembered that Lincoln made a joke regarding Stephens's attire. It was cold and damp weather, and Stephens suffered from the cold. A man of small stature and weighing about ninety pounds, he was described as having on a gray woolen overcoat which came down nearly to his feet, a long wool muffler, and several shawls. Lincoln remarked: "Never have I seen so small a nubbin come out of so much husk."

Grant remembered Lincoln asking him later if he had seen Stephens's overcoat. Grant said yes, and Lincoln said, "Well, didn't you think it was the biggest shuck and the littlest ear that you ever did see?"

The entire meeting was cordial. On their arrival, the commissioners were sent three bottles of whiskey by Seward, although he was aware that Stephens never took more than a teaspoon of it at a time. Hunter asked Seward about the

---

[4]Emil Ludwig, *Abraham Lincoln*, trans. Eden and Cedar Paul (Boston: Little, Brown, and Co., 1930) 112.

capital where Hunter had spent most of his life. Stephens and Lincoln talked of the old days in Congress, and then Stephens put the question, "Mr. President, is there no way of putting an end to the present trouble?"

Lincoln replied that he knew of only one way and that was for those who were resisting the laws of the Union to cease that resistance. Stephens remembered Lincoln as adding, "All the trouble came from armed resistance against the national authority."

One story, perhaps apocryphal, was that Lincoln pulled an envelope from his pocket and wrote thereon the word "Union" and said to his old friend Stephens, "You write the other terms."

Alluding to Blair's Mexican proposition, Stephens asked if there might not be a continental question on which they could adjust the strife. Lincoln rejoined that Blair had spoken on no authority from him.

The discussions were temperate and conciliatory within the context of President Lincoln's fundamental thesis. At one point, according to Stephens, Lincoln said it had not been his intention in the beginning to interfere with slavery, that he had favored no extension of slavery into the territories, and that he did not think the federal government had power over slavery in the states except as a war measure. He had always been in favor of emancipation but not immediate emancipation. Stephens remembered Lincoln saying that the people of the North were as responsible for slavery as the people of the South and that he knew of some in the North who were in favor of an appropriation as high as $400,000,000 for paying owners for the loss of their slaves.

Hunter stated that Lincoln's terms would force the Confederate people into unconditional surrender and submission. Seward insisted that no such words had been used and that peace would place the Southern people under the Constitution, with all their rights secured thereby.

Campbell had the feeling that Stephens, along with Davis, had been duped by Blair into the hopes of somehow interjecting the Mexican question.

Senator Hunter urged a negotiated peace, citing as a parallel the negotiations of King Charles I of England with persons in arms against his government. Lincoln replied:

> Upon questions of history I must refer you to Mr. Seward, for he is posted in such things, and I don't pretend to be bright. My only distinct recollection of the matter is that Charles lost his head.[5]

Lincoln reiterated that the abandonment of armed resistance on the part of the Confederates was an indispensable condition to ending the war. With respect to slavery, he stated that he would not retract or modify the Emancipation Proclamation nor would he return to slavery any person freed by that proclamation or by any Act of Congress. Mr. Seward said there were about 200,000 slaves who had been freed under the actual operation of the proclamation and that the disposition of others would be left to the judiciary or to the Thirteenth Amendment which was then pending. He remarked that the Northern people were weary of the war and that he believed that they would be willing to pay an indemnity for freed slaves.

---

[5] As reported by Francis Bicknell Carpenter in *Six Months at the White House with Abraham Lincoln. The Story of a Picture* (New York: Hurd and Houghton, 1866) reissued by Hurd and Houghton in 1867 as *The Inner Life of Abraham Lincoln. Six Months at the White House.* The story is told by another author that Lincoln added, "And I have no head to spare."

Stephens remembered Lincoln as pausing for some time, his head bent down as if in deep reflection, then rising and saying:

> Stephens, if I were in Georgia, and entertained the sentiments I do—though, I suppose, I should not be permitted to stay there long with them; but if I resided in Georgia, with my present sentiments, I'll tell you what I would do, if I were in your place: I would go home and get the governor of the state to call the legislature together and get them to recall all the state troops from the war; elect senators and members to Congress, and ratify this constitutional amendment *prospectively*, so as to take effect—say in five years. Such a ratification would be valid in my opinion. I have looked into the subject and think such a prospective ratification would be valid. Whatever may have been the views of your people before the war, they must be convinced now, that slavery is doomed. It cannot last long in any event, and the best course it seems to me for your public men to pursue would be to adopt such a policy as will avoid, as far as possible, the evils of immediate emancipation. This would be my course if I were in your place.[6]

After some four hours, the conference concluded with President Lincoln saying he would put the whole matter in the hands of General Grant, with whom the commissioners could interchange views later. Stephens made one last request that Lincoln reconsider the subject of an armistice on the basis of Blair's Mexican proposition. Lincoln replied that he would reconsider it but did not think his mind would change.

As they prepared to leave, Lincoln said to Stephens: "Well, Stephens, there has been nothing we could do for our country. Is there anything I can do for you personally?"

---

[6]*The Lincoln Reader*, ed. Paul M. Angle (New York: De Capo Press, 1947) 502-503.

Stephens replied, "Nothing, unless you can send me my nephew who has been for twenty months a prisoner on Johnson's Island."

Lincoln's face brightened and he said, "I shall be glad to do it. Let me have his name." And he wrote it down in a notebook.

After handshakes, the Confederate commissioners were put in rowboats and taken to the steamer to be taken to their own army lines. They were getting ready to steam away when they saw a rowboat with a black servant at the oars heading for their steamer. He reached their deck with a basket of champagne and a note with the compliments of Secretary Seward. They read the note and waved their handkerchiefs in acknowledgment. In the words of Sandburg, they saw Mr. Seward, speaking through a trumpet, and heard him say in an apparent attempt at humor, "Keep the champagne, but return the negro."

Thus ended the Hampton Roads Peace Conference.

President Lincoln returned to Washington and reported to the Cabinet on 5 February at an evening session. He had spent most of the day writing a message and proclamation to the Senate and the House asking that he be empowered to pay $400,000,000 to the Southern states to be distributed among them pro rata to their respective slave population as shown by the census of 1860 on the condition that all resistance to the national authority be abandoned on or before the first day of April next. He proposed a proclamation looking to peace and reunion, saying that the war cease, the armies reduce to a basis of peace, all political offenses be pardoned, and all property except slaves, which was liable to confiscation or forfeiture, be released.

He laid his resolution and proclamation before the Cabinet. It was unanimously rejected by the Cabinet. Lincoln stated that the war was costing $3,000,000 per day besides all of the lives, but added, "But you are all opposed to me, and I will not send the message."

On the back of the manuscript of his proposed message under the date of 5 February 1865, Lincoln wrote: "Today these papers, which explain themselves, were drawn up and submitted to the Cabinet and unanimously disapproved by them." He signed his name as though the rejection was history and should be of record.

Stephens reported that there was much disappointment over their failure at Hampton Roads. Davis blamed the failure on the fall of Fort Fisher in North Carolina, which fort had prevented the blockade of the Port of Wilmington, virtually the only port left to the Confederates. Davis had no way of knowing Lincoln's own frustration in attempting to bring about peace.

The spirit of the peace conference had been one of reconciliation. The hands of the commissioners were tied by the restriction on their authority to the Mexican ploy and to the insistence on negotiations between separate countries. Lincoln's recorded objective of political pardons, release of property, and indemnity for freeing the slaves upon cessation of hostilities and return of the Confederate states to the Union was blocked by his own Cabinet.

Davis determined to defend Richmond, and Stephens left for Georgia on 9 February to await the end which he considered near.

Lt. John A. Stephens of Georgia was ordered released from Johnson's Island and told to report to President Lincoln at the White House. As he was ushered into his office, President Lincoln rose and said, "I saw your uncle, the Honorable Alexander A. Stephens, recently at Hampton Roads and told him that I would send you to him."

Young Stephens was given the freedom of the city by the president as long as he pleased to remain and was told that he could pass through the lines whenever he was ready to go home. Lincoln talked to him for about an hour about Hampton Roads and about the war. Lt. Stephens stayed in Washington for about two weeks and then reported to President Lincoln that he was ready to go. President Lincoln gave him a letter to carry to his uncle. It read:

> According to our agreement, your nephew, Lieutenant Stephens, goes to you bearing this note. Please, in return, to select and send to me that officer of the same rank imprisoned at Richmond, whose physical condition most urgently requires his release.[7]

As Lincoln signed the pass through the Union army lines for Lt. Stephens, he handed him a photograph of himself and remarked, "You had better take that along. It is considered quite a curiosity down your way, I believe."

April and May of 1865 were eventful months. Lee surrendered to Grant at Appomattox Courthouse on 9 April. President Lincoln was assassinated on 14 April, dying early the next morning. Johnston surrendered to Sherman on 26 April. Davis was arrested on 10 May as he fled through Georgia and was placed in chains at Fort Monroe. Stephens was arrested on 11 May at his home in Crawfordville and taken to Fort Warren near Boston. And Reconstruction began.

---

[7]*Abraham Lincoln: Complete Works*, 2 vols., ed. John G. Nicolay and John Hay (New York: Century Co., 1907) 2:651.

Chapter 10

Lee's Surrender to Grant
Winning and Losing[1]

Introductory Note

The 1990 Public Television program on the Civil War, which was written and produced by Ken Burns and with Shelby Foote as the chief commentator, reminded me that I had Foote's three-volume history of the Civil War in my library.[2] I had once studied the surrender of General Lee to General Grant as he depicted it in the third volume. The television series renewed my interest in the Civil War and especially in Shelby Foote, whose history is filled with anecdotes, many humorous, just as one would suspect from what he had to say in the television series.

Incidentally, everything in this paper is taken from Foote's history or from Winston Churchill's *A History of the English-Speaking Peoples*.[3] in his treatment of our Civil War and Reconstruction. Churchill had a low regard for Grant the president, but had a higher regard for him as a general and the highest regard for his conduct in the surrender of Lee.

Volumes have been written about the war, but Foote writes in a style that is elegant, and he includes a sufficient number of human interest anecdotes to enable one to have a feeling of being there. The surrender of Lee to Grant gives a view of Grant which I never knew of until I read Foote's history. Frankly, I have never heard

---

[1]Editor's note. Judge Bell originally presented this paper to The Ten on 31 January 1991.

[2]Shelby Foote, *The Civil War, a Narrative*, 3 vols. (New York: Random House, 1958–1974).

[3]Winston Churchill, *A History of the English-Speaking Peoples*, 4 vols. (New York: Dodd, Mead, 1956–1958). Churchill treats the American Civil War in vol. 4, *The Great Democracies*.

much good in Grant's favor, but that could be an accident of geography, since I am from the South.

On Tuesday, 8 March 1864, "a short, round-shouldered man in a very tarnished major general's uniform" accompanied by a boy of thirteen sought a room at the Willard Hotel in Washington. The clerk almost turned them away, seeing nothing unusual about the general as contrasted with more than 500 other Union Army generals who had checked in and out of the Willard at various other times during the war. He decided, nevertheless, to give him a room, mainly because of his two stars, and the person checked in as "U. S. Grant & son—Galena, Illinois."

It developed that Grant had been summoned to Washington by President Lincoln to promote him to the newly created rank of Lieutenant General. Grant attended a reception at the White House and was given his additional star the next day by the president. He asked the president what he could do for him and the president said, "I brought you here to take command of all of the Union armies and to capture Richmond."

Grant replied that he would do his best.

Grant left almost immediately to visit the Union armies in Virginia. He went by train to Brandy, some sixty miles from Washington, and visited with General Meade. He had decided that Meade lacked the killer instinct because of his conduct at Gettysburg when he allowed General Lee and his armies to escape at a point where the war could have been ended. After meeting with Meade, he decided not to remove him, but returned to Washington.

President Lincoln sent Grant a message while he was in Virginia advising that Mrs. Lincoln was having a dinner party in his honor on the following Sunday evening. Grant, upon returning to Washington, declined the invitation to be the honoree at the dinner, and when President Lincoln protested,

Grant expressed his appreciation but said that time is very important now, and he added, "Frankly, Mr. Lincoln, I have had enough of this show business."[4]

At the beginning of the campaign, Grant had no geographical objective in mind. His preliminary instructions to Meade, for instance, were "Lee's army will be your objective point. Wherever Lee goes, there you will go also." This instruction was in writing and was dated 9 April 1864. By chance, it was exactly one year later when General Grant notified Secretary of War Stanton as follows:

April 9, 1865—4:30 p.m.

Hon. E. M. Stanton
Secretary of War

General Lee surrendered the Army of Northern Virginia this afternoon upon the terms proposed by myself. The accompanying additional correspondence will show the conditions fully.

U. S. Grant
Lieutenant General

This was half of the Grant plan for ending the war. The other half was to be handled by his chief lieutenant in the campaign to capture the West, General William T. Sherman. Sherman was in Tennessee, and he was told to march into Georgia, defeat the army of General Joseph Johnson, and then hook up with Meade in Virginia. All other operations were curtailed, and Grant ordered the ratio between line troops and

---

[4]Grant was never much on military pomp. One reason: he was tone deaf, and military music was especially annoying to him. He once told a reporter: "I only know two tunes. One of them is Yankee Doodle and the other isn't." As reported by Paul F. Boller, Jr., *Presidential Anecdotes* (New York: Oxford University Press, 1981) 161.

garrison troops to be changed from two-in-garrison to one-on-the-line to a ratio of one-to-one.

With this plan in place, the issue was drawn. There were many battles, and finally Petersburg and Richmond fell. Meanwhile, Sherman had prevailed in Georgia, presented Savannah to President Lincoln as a Christmas 1864 present, and headed north through the Carolinas toward Virginia.

Although Petersburg fell and then Richmond within less than two weeks of Lee's surrender, Grant still had his eye on Lee's army. Lee's army left the Richmond area and headed west toward Appomattox Station. Grant's forces headed in the same direction on a northwesterly course, and the battle was joined in the Appomattox Station area.

The war had turned into one of attrition. Churchill noted the Northern losses, their much larger number of troops, and Grant's aim to end the war as quickly as possible, even if it had to be by attrition. Churchill said that Grant's main strategy as a general was attrition, and it worked. (The population of the Union was more than twice that of the Confederacy.)

Grant had an unusual side to him, as reported by the young lady he later married and to whom he wrote from Mexico during a lull in that war. He said in his letter, "If we have to fight, I would like to do it all at once and then make friends."

Apparently, he felt even more this way, according to Foote, now that the former enemies were his fellow countrymen. His grand plan, or as Foote called it, "Grand Design," was to pull all of the troops together, put them in one plan rather than losing by dividing forces, where reinforcements were not available, as had been the case in several of the greatest Confederate triumphs from the First Bull Run to Chickamauga.

Grant said that "there would be no peace that would be stable and conducive to the happiness of the people, both North and South, until the military power of the rebellion was entirely broken."

He would work toward unconditional surrender. He sought to destroy the means of resistance of his adversaries and also the will to resist. He was not unlike Sherman, who replied to the complaint of a Southern matron about the cruelty of war, "War is cruelty. There is no use trying to reform it. The crueler it is, the sooner it will be over."

The area around Appomattox had hardly been touched by the war; peach trees were in bloom and fields had been plowed for the coming crops. General Fitzhugh Lee had reported to General Lee, his uncle, that the enemy infantry was about four miles away and that the Blue cavalry was not pressing.

The campaign had reached the point where the key was who would get control of the James River west of Richmond. If Lee could round the headwaters of the Appomattox first, he could feed his men from the supply trains he had ordered sent to Appomattox Station, then press on the next day to take shelter behind the James River. If, on the other hand, the Federals got there in time to seize his provisions and to block his path across the twelve-mile headwaters, the campaign would be over.

The Confederate troops, or at least some of the officers, were apparently talking about a surrender, because some of the officers requested General Pendleton to communicate their view to Lee that they must soon surrender and, as General Edward Alexander of Georgia put it, "allow the odium of making the first proposition to be placed upon them," rather than on Lee.

Alexander of Georgia, who was an artillerist, had seen the impending problem clearly and had said that there was but one outlet, the neck of the jug, meaning the headwaters of the Appomattox at Appomattox Station. Both armies were headed there, and, as Alexander said, "Grant had the shortest road."

The group of officers who were to make the proposition to Lee through General Pendleton had not discussed the matter with Generals Longstreet or Gordon, and they refused to join in the message. General Longstreet said angrily, "If General Lee doesn't know when to surrender until I tell him, he will never know."

Grant was meeting on a Saturday afternoon not far away near Farmville with two of his generals, Ord and Gibbon. Gibbon reported later that Grant in "his quiet way, remarked, 'I have a great mind to summon Lee to surrender.' " He called at once for ink and paper and began to write accordingly.

> Headquarters Armies of the United States
> April 7, 1865—5 p.m.
>
> General R. E. Lee
> Commanding C. S. Army
>
> General: The results of the last week must convince you of the hopelessness of further resistance on the part of the Army of Northern Virginia in this struggle. I feel that it is so, and regard it as my duty to shift from myself the responsibility of any further effusion of blood by asking of you the surrender of that portion of the C. S. Army known as the Army of Northern Virginia.
>
> Very respectfully, your obedient servant,
>
> U. S. Grant, Lieutenant General
> Commanding Armies of the United States

Grant charged his inspector general, Brigadier General Seth Williams, with delivery of the message under a flag of truce.

Meanwhile, on the Confederate side, Captain H. H. Perry, adjutant of the brigade sent by Longstreet to reinforce the left, went forward around 9:00 in the evening to investigate a report that a flag of truce had been advanced by the enemy. Captain Perry proceeded with caution because a previous courier had caused gunfire. The young Georgia captain picked his way carefully to a point some fifty yards in front of the lines where he stopped amid a scattering of blue-clad dead and wounded, hit in the last assault, and called for the flag. There then appeared before him, resplendent in the light of the rising moon, what he later described as a "very handsomely dressed Federal officer," who introduced himself as Brigadier General Seth Williams of Grant's staff.

Highly conscious of the contrast they presented, no less in looks than in rank, Perry said, "The truth is, I had not eaten two ounces in two days and I had my coattail then full of corn waiting to parch it as soon as the opportunity might present itself." Perry said that, nevertheless, "I drew myself up as proudly as I could and put on the appearance as well as possible of being perfectly satisfied with my personal exterior."

Once the formalities were out of the way, Williams, who had served as Adjutant at West Point when General Lee was Superintendent there, produced a handsome silver flask and remarked, as Perry afterwards recalled, "that he hoped I would not think it an unsoldierly courtesy if he offered me some very fine brandy." Foote, as he tells this story, said that Perry very much wanted to partake of the brandy, but he said later, "worn down, hungry and dispirited as I was, it would have been a gracious godsend if some old Confederate and I could have emptied that flask between us in that dreadful hour of misfortune. But I raised myself about an inch higher, if possible, bowed and refused politely, trying to produce the ridiculous appearance of having feasted on champagne and pound cake not ten minutes before." General Williams then returned the flask unopened to his pocket and gave Captain Perry the letter from Grant to Lee together with a request for its prompt delivery. Each then bowed profoundly at each other and turned away, each toward his own lines.

A courier soon reached Lee's headquarters in the cottage near Cumberland Church, where he was meeting with General Longstreet. It was close to 10:00 p.m., and Longstreet watched as Lee studied the message. He later said that there was no emotion in Lee's face and he passed the message to Longstreet without comment. Longstreet read the surrender request, then handed it back. Lee said, "Not yet."

Lee then wrote his answer to Grant on a single sheet of paper and gave it to the courier to be sent across the lines.

7th Apl '65

Genl

I have recd your note of this date. Though not entertaining the opinion you express of the hopelessness of further resistance on the part of the Army of N. Va. I reciprocate your desire to avoid useless effusion of blood, & therefore before considering your proposition, ask the terms you will offer on condition of its surrender.

> Very respy your obt Svt,
> R. E. Lee, Genl

Lt Genl U. S. Grant
Commd Armies of the U States

A few hours later Pendleton approached Lee with the message from the officers of suggested surrender and Lee heard him out, but said nothing of Grant's message or of his own reply. In fact, by requesting terms of Grant, he had already begun the negotiations that General Pendleton was recommending. He even demurred to the Pendleton proposition, saying, "I trust it has not come to that."

This convinced Alexander that Lee "preferred himself to take the whole responsibility of surrender, as he had always taken that of his battles." The Confederate army continued to march and reached Appomattox Courthouse, some three miles short of Appomattox Station, by dark.

As the Confederates were making camp, a courier brought another message to Lee. Lee opened the message as Gordon and Longstreet watched. Grant's reply was that

> Peace being my great desire, there is but one condition I would insist upon—namely, that the men and officers surrendered shall be disqualified from taking up arms against the Government of the United States until properly exchanged.

Foote points out that not only was this a far cry from the "unconditional" demand that had won Grant his *nom de guerre* in the battle at Fort Donaldson, but Grant considerably added:

> I will meet you or will designate officers to meet any officers you may name for the same purpose, at any point agreeable to you, for the purpose of arranging definitely the terms upon which the surrender of the Army of Northern Virginia will be received.

Foote writes that nothing of Lee's reaction showed in his face. "How would you answer that?" Lee asked of an aide, who read it and replied, "I would answer no such letter." Lee replied, "Ah, but it must be answered," and by the flickering light of a candle, he proceeded to do so.

> In mine of yesterday, I did not intend to propose the surrender of the Army of N. Va. but asked the terms of your proposition. To be frank, I do not think that the emergency has risen to call for surrender of this army, but as a restoration of peace should be the sole object of all, I desire to know whether your proposals would lead to that end. I cannot therefore meet you with a view to surrender the Army of N. Va.; but as far as your

proposal may affect the C. S. forces under my command, and tend to the restoration of peace, I shall be pleased to meet you at 10:00 a.m. tomorrow on the Old Stage Road to Richmond between the picket lines of the two armies.

As his courier left, the artillery erupted and General Pendleton, a former Episcopal rector, reported that sixty pieces were in place awaiting the resumption of the march on the next day. He said that all seemed well until a sudden attack by Union cavalry exploded out of the twilight woods, fully in the faces of the lounging cannoniers. Two batteries were ordered to hold off the Blue troopers while the rest pulled back, and there ensued what a participant called "one of the closest artillery fights in the time it lasted that occurred during the war. The guns were fought literally up to the muzzles." Shortly thereafter, Pendleton replied that he feared that half of his guns had been lost, including those in the two batteries left behind. Lee then learned that the supply trains, which had been ordered to wait, had also been captured. Information also came that there were heavy Union forces in the twelve-mile watershed that had to be crossed to reach the James.

Lee summoned Generals Longstreet and Gordon and Fitzhugh Lee to his headquarters. Lee stood by a fire that had been kindled against the chill, explained the tactical situation, as far as he knew it, and read them Grant's two letters, together with his replies. Then he did something he had not done, at least in this collective way, since the eve of the Seven Days' Battle, shortly after he took over as their leader. He asked for their advice. "We knew by our own aching hearts that his was breaking," Gordon was to say, "yet he commanded himself, and stood calmly facing and discussing the long-dreaded inevitable."

They decided to continue fighting and would try for a breakout and a getaway westward toward Appomattox

Station and the headwaters. Gordon would take the lead and Longstreet's corps would bring up the rear. Gordon pointed out that it was a long-odds gamble at best and that "the utmost that could be hoped for was that we might reach the mountains of Virginia and Tennessee with a remnant of the army, and ultimately join General Johnson" (who had escaped Sherman, although with heavy losses).

Meanwhile, Grant was bedded down some fifteen miles to the east in an upstairs room of a deserted house, but not asleep. He had a splitting headache. Grant had wired Secretary of War Stanton that "I feel very confident of receiving the surrender of Lee and what remains of his army tomorrow." He stated that his terms were too generous for his opponent to decline in his present condition. He had waited some eight hours for Lee's reply, and the blinding headache struck him just as the sun was going down.

At 10:00, a dispatch from General Sheridan arrived, saying that his cavalrymen had reached Appomattox Station at dusk, ahead of the leading elements of Lee's army. He reported that he had captured the supply trains which were waiting for the hungry Confederates and had established a dug-in position athwart the Lynchburg Road, blocking Lee's escape in the only direction that mattered. He thought that they would finish the job on General Lee on the next day and suggested that he did not think Lee meant to surrender until he was compelled to do so.

Lee's message arrived shortly after Sheridan's. Grant studied the note, more saddened than angered about what he discerned, and shook his head. "It looks as if Lee means to fight," he said.

Grant's staff was outraged by Lee's reply, but Grant remained calm. Grant defended his year-long adversary, protesting that in his present "trying position" the old warrior was "compelled to defer somewhat to the wishes of his government. . . . But it all means precisely the same. If I meet Lee he will surrender before I leave."

One of his generals said he had no right to meet with Lee or even to arrange terms of peace and that this was the prerogative of the president or the Senate. Grant yielded, but insisted that he must still do Lee the courtesy of answering his letter, if only to decline the suggested meeting. "I will reply in the morning," he said.

At dawn, Grant wrote Lee:

> Your note of yesterday is received. I have no authority to treat on the subject of peace; the meeting proposed for 10:00 a.m. today could lead to no good. I will state, however, General, that I am equally anxious for peace with yourself and the whole North entertains the same feeling. The terms upon which peace can be had are well understood. By the South laying down their arms they will hasten that most desirable event, save thousands of human lives, and hundreds of millions of property not yet destroyed. Seriously hoping that all our difficulties may be settled without loss of another life, I subscribe myself,
>
> U. S. Grant, Lieutenant General

The note was delivered, and a few hours later Grant received Lee's reply. He read it with no expression on his face, and one of his generals said, "You had better read it aloud, General." Whereupon Grant did so in a deep voice that was by now a little shaky with emotion. Lee's letter was as follows:

> April 9th, 1865
>
> General: I received your note of this morning on the picket line, whither I had come to meet you and ascertain definitely what terms were embraced in your proposal of yesterday with reference to the surrender of this army. I now request an interview, in accordance with the offer contained in your letter of yesterday, for that purpose.

Very respectfully, Your obt servt
R. E. Lee

Foote writes that the celebration that followed was unexpectedly subdued. Most throats were too constricted for speech, let alone cheers. "All felt that the war was over. Every heart was thinking of friends—family—home." Grant was the first to recover his voice, his headache cured as if in reaction. Negotiations were back on the track, and the track was Grant's.

Foote writes that Lee had foreseen the outcome from the start, and showed it when he joined the staff around the campfire that morning, a couple of hours before daylight, dressed in a splendid new gray uniform. His boots were highly polished, and he had buckled on his sword with the ornate hilt and scabbard. Pendleton expressed surprise, and Lee said, "I have probably to be General Grant's prisoner, and I thought I must make my best appearance."

The fighting had been heavy that morning, and finally Gordon decided that he had to pull back if he was to avoid being cut off and annihilated. He kept up the fire, but sent a message to General Lee when the staff colonel arrived to inquire how things were going. "Tell General Lee how I fought my corps to a frazzle and I fear I can do nothing unless I am heavily supported by Longstreet."

Lee received the message the next morning without flinching, though he saw clearly what it meant. If so stalwart a fighter as Gordon could "do nothing" without the help of Longstreet, then he had lost all choice in the matter. Lee then said to his staff, "Then there is nothing left me to do but go to see General Grant, and I would rather die a thousand deaths." This was the morning that he was to meet General Grant between the picket lines.

General Alexander, a West Pointer, aged 30, suggested that the army could avoid capture if it disbanded and dispersed. Lee heard the young brigadier out and then replied in measured tones:

> We must consider its effect on the country as a whole. Already it is demoralized by the four years of war. If I took your advice, men would be without rations and under no control of officers. They would be compelled to rob and steal in order to live. They would become mere bands of marauders, and the enemy's cavalry could pursue them and overrun many sections they may never have occasion to visit. We would bring on a state of affairs that would take the country years to recover from. And as for myself, young fellows might go bushwacking, but the only dignified course for me would be to go to General Grant and surrender myself and take the consequences of my acts.

Alexander was silenced, then and down the years. He wrote long afterwards: "I had not a single word to say in reply. He answered my suggestion from a plane so far above it that I was ashamed of having made it."

As Lee prepared to attend the 10:00 meeting with Grant, he received Grant's notice that there would be no meeting. Lee then knew that there had to be an unconditional surrender, and he then dictated the message which Grant had received. While waiting for further word from Grant, Lee sent General Gordon a note authorizing him to request a similar truce of the enemy moving against him from the opposite direction. Sheridan did not want to give the cease-fire but was overruled by General Ord.

As the Confederate officers awaited word from Grant, someone thought that Grant would stiffen his terms. Lee said not. He had been well acquainted with Grant for years before the war and he did not believe that Grant would demand anything that Lee would not demand if the roles were reversed.

Grant answered Lee's letter by saying he was pushing forward and asked Lee to advise where the interview would take place. Lee's aide, Colonel Marshall, was sent to find a suitable place.

The interview—a polite term used by Grant and Lee instead of "surrender"—took place in a brick house at Appomattox Courthouse owned by a man named Wilmer McLean, who had agreed that it could be so used.

Lee arrived first. As Grant approached, he was met by General Sheridan. Grant asked the whereabouts of Lee, and Sheridan replied, "He is up there in that brick house." Grant replied, "Very well. Let's go up." Grant entered and went at once to Lee, who rose to meet him.

* * *

In the third volume of his *The Civil War, a Narrative*, Shelby Foote brings to a close the story of four years of turmoil and strife that altered American life forever.[5] (The loss of life alone was astronomical: the war had resulted in more than 630,000 dead and more than one million casualties.) Foote describes in much detail the meeting of Lee with Grant. The meeting lasted about an hour and a half. At the end, the surrender of the Army of Northern Virginia allowed the Federal government to bring increased pressure to bear in other parts of the South that resulted in the surrender, over the next few months, of the remaining armies of the Confederacy. Grant had written the terms of surrender in a letter from himself to Lee. The terms were generous and allowed the former Confederates to disengage and go home feeling they had been treated with dignity and respect.

---

[5]Volume 3 was entitled *Red River to Appomattox*.

Deftly summarizing the events of the end of the war, Winston Churchill—who himself knew much of war—wrote this about the surrender and Grant:

> When there were no more half-rations of green corn and roots to give to the soldiers, and they were beset on three sides, Grant ventured to appeal to Lee to recognize that his position was hopeless. Lee bowed to physical necessity. He rode on Traveller to Appomattox Court House to learn what terms would be offered. Grant wrote them out in a few sentences. The officers and men of the Army of Northern Virginia must surrender their arms and return on parole to their homes, not to be molested while they observed the laws of the United States. Lee's officers were to keep their swords. Food would be provided from the Union wagons. Grant added, "Your men must keep their horses and mules. They will need them for the spring ploughing." This was the greatest day in the career of General Grant, and stands high in the story of the United States. The Army of Northern Virginia which so long had "carried the Confederacy on its bayonet," surrendered, twenty-seven thousand strong; and a fortnight later, despite the protests of President Davis, Johnston accepted from Sherman terms similar to those granted to Lee. Davis himself was captured by a cavalry squadron. The armed resistance of the Southern states was thus entirely subdued.[6]

Grant and Lee demonstrated a wisdom beyond that of their subordinates, and in Lee's case beyond his superiors. First, Grant, a fighting general who sacrificed tens of thousands of the North's sons to wear down his opponent, rightly saw that the one important goal by 9 April 1865 was to get Lee's army off the field. Imprisonments of Confederate officers could have been popular, even justified. Confiscation

---

[6]From vol. 4 (*The Great Democracies*) of Churchill's *A History of the English-Speaking Peoples* (New York: Dodd, Mead, 1956–1958).

of all horses and stock would have been authorized and expected. Parading Lee down the streets of Washington would have been a victor's right. But Grant knew such actions could have engendered guerilla resistance in the South and reprisals in the North. "Unconditional Surrender" Grant saw that "surrender" was more important than "conditions" or even vengeance.

Second, Lee, a relentless general who always found an escape and who, like Grant, sent tens of thousands to their deaths, saw that relent he must. Lee, the quintessential West Point gentleman, saw no dishonor in admitting defeat and in accepting the responsibility for it. At no point after the surrender did Lee curse the Union or blame the Confederate government for the loss of his army. Lee recognized that continuing the real fight, or figuratively refighting the war, served no good purpose. Ironically, Lee, like Grant, wanted to get the Army of Northern Virginia off the field of battle. Perhaps Lee's wisdom in this regard came because he never fought for "the Cause." Lee fought for his soldiers. Once he saw that his men could never win and never escape, Lee moved quickly toward surrender.

These preeminent soldiers, then, showed themselves to be statesmen, too. Being gracious in victory, taking responsibility for defeat—timeless tactics to ending wars—worked to great advantage at Appomattox Court House.

Chapter 11

A Kind Word for General Sherman
The Limits of Military Action[1]

The eighty-one days of 2 February through 24 April 1865 were the testing time in bringing the Civil War to a successful conclusion. First came the so-called Peace Conference between President Lincoln and Secretary of State Seward, on one side, and Alex Stephens, vice president of the Confederacy, as well as Senator Hunter and former Supreme Court Justice Campbell on the other. This Peace Conference took place at Hampton Roads, Virginia, 2-3 February.

Then came four other events that, together with the first, constitute one of the most determinative periods in our country's existence. The first of these four events was the meeting between President Lincoln and Generals Grant and Sherman at City Point, Virginia during the period 24 March to 8 April 1865.

This was followed by the surrender at Appomattox on 9 April by General Lee to General Grant. Then followed the assassination of President Lincoln on 14 April and the surrender of General Johnston in North Carolina to General Sherman during the period 14 to 24 April.

We have touched on the roles of Lincoln, Grant, and Lee in bringing the war to a close. We turn now to General Sherman to see him in a light quite different from how he has been viewed by the average white Southerner in the years following the Civil War.

---

[1]Editor's note. Judge Bell prepared this paper for The Ten in November 2006.

Lincoln made it clear at the Peace Conference that the future of the Confederate States resided in those states ceasing participation in the war and rejoining the Union. Each such state would have all of the rights afforded the other states in the Union.

Upon returning to Washington, Lincoln gave a report to his Cabinet and attempted, as an incentive to settlement, to have the Cabinet authorize four hundred million dollars to be paid for freeing the slaves. Not one Cabinet member would agree, and the idea was abandoned. At this point, it was clear that the war had to be fought to the end.

President Lincoln summoned General Grant and later General Sherman to meet with him at City Point, Virginia to discuss the prospect of ending the war, what would be done with the military of the Confederacy, and how to restore governments in the several Confederate states.

City Point is on the James River some twenty miles east of and below Richmond. It was a depot and staging area for the Union army. President Lincoln arrived by boat via the Chesapeake Bay and the James River. He was at City Point from 24 March to 8 April, the day before Lee's surrender. He toured battlefields and even Richmond after it fell, as well as having meetings with Generals Grant and Sherman.

Questions as to civil matters were reserved for President Lincoln, while military matters were left to Generals Grant and Sherman. But Lincoln's plan, as he suggested to Grant and Sherman, was to let the resisters off lightly so as to restore the Union. He even suggested that it would suit him if Jefferson Davis were to escape to another country.

The surrender of General Lee was contemplated to take place at an early date, and it was thought that General Sherman was near the point of defeating the forces of General Johnston in North Carolina. The danger of the Confederate forces being converted into guerilla operations was very much on the minds of all three. They had the example of the victories by the state militia in North and South Carolina against the British in the Revolutionary War, as well as guerilla operations following wars in other lands.

Indeed, at the same moment some of General Lee's staff wanted to do just that. However, General Lee disagreed and would have no part in it. He said that enough harm had been done to the country as it was.

The Army of General Johnston—one hundred thousand strong—was another matter. Lee and Johnston attempted to join forces, but that effort failed because General Grant's army overwhelmed General Lee before he could reach North Carolina and General Johnston.

Lee surrendered on 9 April at Appomattox, Virginia and received magnanimous treatment at the hands of General Grant, much as President Lincoln had suggested at the City Point meeting. It was Lincoln's idea that the Confederate soldiers would be allowed to return home to civilian pursuits and would not be punished once they took an oath to support the United States. They had to turn in their arms and battle flags and were then free to go. As stated, President Lincoln had made it clear, at least to Grant, that the military was not to be involved in political questions as part of the surrender, such as reestablishing civilian government in the surrendering states.

Meanwhile, beginning on 14 April, just days after Lee's surrender, General Sherman was discussing terms of surrender with General Johnston at the request of General Johnston, who, incidentally, was defying the orders of President Davis not to surrender.

Sherman advised General Grant and Secretary of War Stanton by telegraph of the offer of surrender from General Johnston and that he would give Johnston the same terms as Grant had given to Lee and would be careful not to implicate any terms of civil policy. Despite this promise, General Sherman almost immediately wandered into the turbulent policy of civil reconstruction which, upon Lincoln's death, was becoming the new order for the Confederate states.

On the morning of 15 April, while on his way to meet with General Johnston to finish the discussion over the terms of surrender, Sherman received word of the assassination of Lincoln the day before when he was handed a telegram from Secretary of War Stanton: "President Lincoln was murdered about 10 o'clock last night."

Sherman moved ahead and on the 18th gave Johnston more favorable terms of surrender than Lee had received. His terms of surrender included two provisions relating to the civil questions which, according to President Lincoln's City Point instruction, were to be left to the President: (1) the president would recognize existing state governments and (2) the former Confederate soldiers would be permitted to vote after taking the oath of allegiance to the Union.

The surrender document was sent to Secretary of War Stanton as well as to General Grant and the cabinet for approval on 21 April 1865. Grant knew immediately that it could not be approved. A fire storm ensued, directed in the press by Secretary Stanton against General Sherman. Stanton was motivated to destroy Sherman, who had become popular and was believed by Stanton to have ambitions of becoming a candidate for president.

Sherman was accused of being in league with the Confederates, among other malfeasances. One claim was that he was a Confederate sympathizer because he had been president of the Louisiana State Institute (now LSU) when he returned to Army service in 1861. He was a West Point graduate and had been a regular Army officer in his prior experience before becoming a railroad president and at one point a lawyer.

To further complicate the situation, upon Lincoln's death, the forces in the national government, including Andrew Johnson, the new president, were intent on visiting harsh punishment on the South, and the cry included threats to recall General Sherman. The upshot was to investigate him for misconduct and dereliction of duty because of the generous terms of surrender and to send General Grant to take over from Sherman.

General Grant calmed the waters by agreeing to take over and to resume fighting with General Johnston. Upon arriving at Johnston's headquarters, he learned that Sherman had already advised Johnston that the surrender had been rejected. The result was that Grant then gave Johnston the same terms as had been given to Lee, and the matter ended.

It developed that the Confederates did not resort to guerilla warfare, but the Union did persist in imposing Reconstruction on the South. The Reconstruction group wanted, among other things, no restrictions on the former slaves voting, but wanted to prohibit white Confederates from voting. This led to more turmoil and bad race relations, but Grant ended up as president in 1869, and he promptly made General Sherman the chief of the Army. Finally, about seven years after the war, the last of the Army of Occupation was removed from the former Confederate states, and President Lincoln's wish that there be a Union of the states was realized.

The surrender events in 1865 left Sherman very bitter. He took his army to Washington to march in the victory parade, although Secretary of War Stanton had tried to stop him and had passed the word for the other generals not to follow Sherman's orders. At the parade, Sherman greeted President Andrew Johnson in the receiving stand, but refused to shake the outstretched hand of Secretary Stanton, who was also in the receiving stand. Sherman also blamed General Halleck, the chief of staff of the Army at the time, and their friendship was never restored.

After the War, Sherman explained why he gave General Johnston such liberal terms by saying that he was worried over who would be in position to govern in the Confederate states and that he thought the best possible leaders would be from the ranks of the Confederate soldiers who had taken the loyalty oaths.

Sherman was in outspoken disagreement with the Reconstruction policies and particularly with giving the former slaves the immediate right to vote. In talking to Chief Justice Chase on 4 May 1865, he explained why he did not favor giving the right to vote to the freed slaves. It would, he argued, revive the war and spread its field of operations. Why not, therefore, trust to the slower but no less sure means of statesmanship? Why not imitate the example of England in allowing causes to work out their gradual solution instead of imitating the French, whose political revolutions had been bloody and had actually retarded the development of political freedom?[2]

General Sherman was opposed to much of the severity of Reconstruction. In addition to his views toward the immediate vote for the freed slaves, he opposed the use of the Army to enforce the laws against the terrorist activities of the Ku Klux Klan.[3] Sherman insisted that the problem would not have arisen if the terms of his surrender proposal had been followed. Some of the harshness in the Reconstruction was ameliorated when President Johnson agreed to let the Confederate soldiers hold state office. The Ku Klux Klan law

---

[2]Stanley P. Hirshson, *The White Tecumseh: A Biography of General William T. Sherman* (New York: J. Wiley, 1997) 314.
[3]See Civil Rights Act of 1871, 28 U.S.C.A. §1343.

was replaced by the Posse Comitatus Act in 1878, effectively ending such use of the Army.[4]

In retrospect, what did cause Sherman to give the favorable terms to General Johnston? One factor may have been to gain Johnston's cooperation. Sherman wanted Johnston to surrender not only his Army but what was left in other states of the Confederate Army, and Johnston agreed. Johnston also appealed to Sherman as an Army officer and an American to help the Confederates in the straits that they were in. One of the straits confronting them was how to assimilate the freed slaves into full citizenship, such as voting.

Sherman's unique background was another possible factor. He viewed himself as a Westerner, which meant the Midwest of the country or the Mississippi Valley, as distinguished from the Eastern part of the country. He considered the soldiers from the West as superior to the Easterners. He had many years of service in the South: Charleston, Florida, and then Louisiana, and the western city of St. Louis was for a long time his choice as a place to live.

He detested the press and considered reporters as a hindrance, as well as a nuisance and even a danger in disclosing information regarding the Army. He also detested politics, although his brother John was a longtime U.S. senator from Ohio.

When Sherman was urged to run for president (one of several times this was suggested), he made the now famous statement:

> Now as to politics, I think all my personal friends know my deep-seated antipathy to the subject; yet, as you seem not to understand me, I hereby state, and mean all that I say, that I HAVE NEVER BEEN AND NEVER WILL BE A CANDIDATE FOR

---

[4] 20 Stat 152; 18 U.S.C.A. §1385.

PRESIDENT; THAT, IF NOMINATED BY EITHER PARTY, I SHOULD PEREMPTORILY DECLINE; AND EVEN IF UNANIMOUSLY ELECTED, I SHOULD DECLINE TO SERVE. If you find language stronger to convey this meaning, you are at liberty to use it.[5]

As to the fortunes of war, in the years after the war, the Civil War generals became friendly and often visited one another at home and at national meetings. Many had known each other at West Point. At one such meeting, General Heth, a Confederate general, is said to have told General Sherman:

> Stop, Sherman, and think. If there are two men in the world that should go on their knees and thank the Almighty for raising up the rebels, those two men are Grant and yourself; but for the rebels you would now be teaching school in the swamps of Louisiana and Grant would be tanning bad leather at Galena.

Placing his hand on Heth's shoulder, Sherman said, "That is so, old fellow.[6]

General Sherman was a quintessential nineteenth-century American. Born in Ohio and educated at West Point, he served several years in the regular Army throughout the country, including in the South and West. Tiring of Army life, he became a lawyer and railroad president, then an educator, as president of the Louisiana Military Institute.

When the Civil War started, Sherman left to join the Union Army, with advice to the South that they were foolish to think that they could win a war against the Union states. He abhorred war because he was a student of war. His method of fighting was extreme on the civilian population, but measured in his judgment by the standard of destroying the will as well as the capacity of the South to fight. (In the lore of Southern—or at least Georgian—humor, it was often

[5]Hirshson, *The White Tecumseh*, 346.
[6]Hirshson, *The White Tecumseh*, 369.

said in the years following the war that Sherman was a fine general, but a little careless with fire.) His conduct was most extreme in South Carolina, which he considered to be the location of the greatest treason to the Union.

However, like President Lincoln and General Grant and, later, Generals Marshall and McArthur, Sherman viewed, as a necessary part of war's end, assisting in the rebuilding of the conquered for a place in the family of states or nations, as the case might be, while avoiding guerilla warfare and insurrection. Thus, the general most hated by whites in the postwar South sought to be the most lenient toward the defeated Confederates.

Chapter 12

Oliver Wendell Holmes

The Rule of Law [1]

Justice Oliver Wendell Holmes (1841–1935) was one of the most important figures in the history of our country. During his lifespan, he served as an officer in the Union Army during the Civil War, a lawyer, a Harvard law professor, many years as a jurist on the Supreme Court of Massachusetts, and thirty years as a justice of the Supreme Court of the United States, retiring at age ninety in 1932. He lived to be ninety-three.[2]

The long life of Justice Holmes shaped the American view of law. Our unusual form of government is founded necessarily on a system of law. Our forefathers brought our law from England in the form of the Common Law as it had been developed there. In his *A History of the English-Speaking Peoples*, Churchill extolled the virtues of the Common Law and considered it one of the greatest contributions of England to the world. The Common Law is to be distinguished from the Roman Law which applies in many non-English-related countries, and even to a large extent in one American state, Louisiana.

---

[1] <u>Editor's note</u>. Judge Bell presented this paper to The Ten on 1 December 2005.

[2] It is hard for us to imagine that a person who served in the Civil War lived into the presidency of President Franklin Delano Roosevelt during the Great Depression, but Justice Holmes did. Shortly after his election, President Roosevelt paid a courtesy call on Justice Holmes at his home. He noticed that Justice Holmes was reading from Plato in Greek. He inquired as to why he was doing so. Justice Holmes replied, "Young man, I am trying to improve my mind." He was 93 at the time.

Justice Benjamin Nathan Cardozo (1870–1938), an eminent jurist in his own right, once described our form of government as a system of "ordered liberty." The very basis of "ordered liberty" owes its genesis to the Common Law as it came to be adopted in our country.

That law, the Common Law, became the foundation of the career of Justice Holmes. But first let us consider Justice Holmes as a man, as a historical American icon and true American patriot.

What kind of person was Justice Holmes and what were his greatest contributions to our system of "ordered liberty"?

A Boston native, Oliver Wendell Holmes graduated from Harvard at age twenty, just at the beginning of the Civil War, and promptly enlisted in the Army as a part of the troops being raised in Massachusetts. After receiving his training in the Army, he became a lieutenant in the 20th Massachusetts. He fought in many battles and was wounded in three: at Ball's Bluff, Antietam, and Fredericksburg. He was wounded in his first battle, Ball's Bluff (also known as the Battle of Harrison's Landing or the Battle of Leesburg), and returned home for recuperation. Returning to the Army, Holmes was severely wounded again, this time at Antietam. It was first thought he was killed, but he survived and was sent home for recuperation. Going back to active duty a third time, he was wounded at Fredericksburg and returned home for a third time for recuperation.[3]

Holmes's enlistment had been for three years, and when it expired in 1865 near the end of the war, he decided to

---

[3]There were no hospitals at the time set aside for those wounded in service to recuperate, as in modern times, and home was the place for recuperation.

pursue graduate education. He was torn between philosophy and law and decided to enter law school.[4]

Holmes's father—a medical doctor, a professor in the Harvard Medical School, and a noted poet—took a dim view of lawyers. When Wendell stated that he had decided to be a lawyer, Dr. Holmes looked up from his desk and asked, "What is the use of that, Wendell? A lawyer can't be a great man." This, coming from a father whose own brother was a lawyer and whose mother's father was a judge. His father's words bothered Wendell Holmes for the rest of his life. He perhaps was driven to prove his father wrong.

Upon completing law school at Harvard, he entered the law practice in 1867, but was more a student of the law than a trial lawyer, and George Shattuck, his senior partner and mentor, early on decided that he probably should have a career as a jurist.[5]

Among Holmes's achievements as a lawyer was his authorship of *The Common Law*, first published in 1881. This book brought the common law, which had existed for several hundred years, up to date and was recognized as a scholarly work of the first order by eminent scholars in both England and in the United States. It was clearly a highly regarded

---

[4]Some of the great men of the nation had been lawyers, particularly "the Founders," John Adams, Jefferson, Madison, Monroe, and John Quincy Adams. They were all trained in the law. Burke had remarked in the Parliament that the American union was governed by lawyers. Alexis de Tocqueville, a young Frenchman writing *Democracy in America* in 1834–1835, reached the same conclusion, remarking that the only aristocracy in America was the legal profession.

[5]Incidentally, the oath that Holmes took upon admission to the bar provided that he would not "wittingly or willingly promote or sue any false, groundless, or unlawful suit nor give aid or consent to the same."

treatise and the result of some ten years of hard work in his spare time.

The subject matter of *The Common Law* consists of several chapters, each of which was drawn from lectures he gave at Harvard.[6]

Holmes's reputation was so enhanced by his authorship and his lectures that he was offered and accepted a teaching position at the Harvard Law School in 1882, but teaching was not to be for him for very long. After a short time at Harvard, he was appointed a justice of the Supreme Court of Massachusetts in 1883 and served there until his appointment to the Supreme Court of the United States in 1902.

Holmes came to the bench in a time of great change in our country. Businesses were becoming large, and there was much labor unrest. His thought was that when the pattern of society changes, legislation must meet the change or the state will perish. In the Common Law, he said, judges must bear in mind public policy, the felt necessities of the time. This became the judicial philosophy of Holmes—his hallmark on the law. There was a mixture of law, philosophy, and his battlefield experience in his thinking as a judge.

In a Memorial Day address in 1894, he answered the question of why people still observed Memorial Day. Holmes remembered his friends and Harvard classmates who had died

---

[6]It is the very nature of the common law that it continues to grow as there are more cases and thus more precedents to follow, or as it is changed by statute. The common law is stable in the sense of discovering what it is at a given time, and because of the doctrine of *stare decisis* ("to stand by decided matters"), but is never static in the sense of not growing. Growth, based on changing conditions, is inherent in the common law concept. Justice Holmes put it well when he said that "The life of the law has not been logic; it has been experience." *The Common Law* (Boston: Little, Brown, and Co., 1881) lecture 1.

in the war and told of their bravery and comradeship.[7] He said:

> Through our great good fortune, in our youth our hearts were touched with fire. It was given to us to learn at the outset that life is a profound and passionate thing. While we were permitted to scorn nothing by indifference, and do not pretend to undervalue the worldly rewards of ambition, we have seen with our own eyes, beyond and above the gold fields, the snowy heights of honor, and it is for us to bear the report to those who come after us. . . .

As a judge, Justice Holmes was his own man. Sometimes he was thought of as a liberal and at other times a conservative. He dissented from time to time, but always in a respectful and reasoned way.

In state cases, he dissented from the holding that a state statute making it a crime to withhold part of an employee's wages for imperfect work was valid. He did not see that such a statute impaired a contract, saying that such a law did not interfere with the right to acquire, possess, or protect property any more than laws against usury or gaming. This was construed as a liberal position.

Again, in another dissent he could find nothing wrong with a statute allowing cities to purchase and sell coal and wood as fuels. He thought it was no more than the power to take land for railroads or laws to support paupers.

Justice Holmes dissented in a labor case where the court enjoined pickets from marching in front of a shop contending that the shop owner was unfair to his workers. Holmes viewed the picketing as pure competition so long as it was

---

[7]Harvard's Union war dead are listed in Memorial Hall. To this day, Confederate dead from Harvard are not memorialized, though Memorial Church lists *German* casualties from World War I.

disassociated from any threat of violence. Like many of his dissents, this position later became the majority view in such contests between management and labor.

In 1902, Vice President Theodore Roosevelt became president when President McKinley was assassinated. Shortly thereafter, Justice Horace Gray of the United States Supreme Court became ill and resigned. Justice Holmes was appointed to his place, but only after President Roosevelt sought to be assured from others that Holmes was in sympathy with his views on antitrust. It is not known whether the president ever sought the personal assurance of Holmes and there is no claim that he did. It is sure that Holmes quickly disappointed President Roosevelt.

Roosevelt was dead set against the big monopolies that had been created in the United States, including Standard Oil, U.S. Steel, American Tobacco, the railroads, and the consolidated banking industry.

The *Northern Securities Co. v. United States* case of 1903, involving railroad consolidations, was pending in the Supreme Court. Roosevelt wanted to prevent the consolidation. This was a Sherman Antitrust Act case, and Holmes felt uncomfortable with the Sherman Act, which, in a letter he once wrote to Sir Frederick Pollock, he called "a humbug based on economic ignorance and incompetence."[8] The Court, in a 5-4 opinion, found the consolidation to be in violation of the Sherman Act. Holmes was with the dissenting four. His dissenting opinion was a great shock to President

---

[8]The Sherman Antitrust Act was the first U.S. government action to limit cartels and monopolies. However, it became controversial, with one branch of criticism contending that, rather than improving competition and benefiting consumers, it merely aided inefficient businesses at the expense of larger, more innovative ones.

Roosevelt. Holmes was joined by three other justices in his dissent.

In response, Roosevelt stated that the justices should follow their conscience. If a court so ruled, in the belief of Justice Holmes, it would be no court at all. To Holmes, the Supreme Court existed for the purpose of interpreting the statutes according to the United States Constitution. The pressure of public opinion only served to cloud the issue. Holmes saw nothing wrong with "bigness" of businesses so long as they did not misuse their size. In other words, he said, size may be reached for other ends than those that make them monopolies.

President Roosevelt was enraged with Justice Holmes and said, as if Holmes had lost his nerve, that "I could carve out of a banana a judge with more backbone than that!"

Holmes later wrote to a friend that Roosevelt looked on his dissent as a political departure which stood in his way. He said it broke up their friendship. When Roosevelt died, Holmes wrote to a friend that "He [Roosevelt] was very likeable, a big figure, a rather ordinary intellect, with extraordinary gifts, a shrewd and I think pretty unscrupulous politician. He played all his cards—if not more. R.I.P."[9]

To Holmes, the times indicated that the government was out to bust the trusts, as the business monopolies were called, but the corporations were out to bust the labor unions and to avoid state statutes protecting the workers. The country was in a period of revolutionary social change.

At this point, in 1905, the Supreme Court heard the *Lochner v. United States* case involving whether the state of New York could prevent bakers from working their employ-

---

[9]As quoted by H. W. Brands, *T.R. The Last Romantic* (New York: Basic Books, 1997) 542.

ees more than ten hours per day. The Court voted 5-4 for the bakery owner, Lochner. In Holmes's dissent, again written for four justices, he said that

> [I]t is settled that state constitutions and state laws may regulate life in many ways which we as legislators might think injudicious . . . but a constitution is not intended to embody a particular theory, whether of paternalism and the organic relation of the citizen to the state or of laissez faire. It is made for people of fundamentally differing views, and the accident of our finding certain opinions natural and familiar or novel and even shocking ought not to conclude our judgment upon the question whether the statutes embodying them conflict with the Constitution of the United States.

At this point, after three years on the Court, Holmes had in *Northern Securities Co.* first taken a position supporting corporations despite their size, if there had been no abuse from the size; now, in *Lochner*, he sided with labor with respect to a statute protecting the laborer.

There is a thread that runs through the opinions of Justice Holmes which shows his skepticism toward the Sherman Act and which led to the Court adopting the rule of reason in construing it. This began in the Standard Oil cases in 1910, when the Court held that Standard Oil was an "unreasonable combination or monopoly." Justice Holmes concurred in the majority opinion written by Justice White, which thereby imported the standard of reasonableness into the Sherman Act.

The other thread has to do with the use of the Fourteenth Amendment against the states. In *Baldwin v. Missouri*, a tax case, the Court struck down the state tax statute, and Holmes dissented. He said, in part:

> I have not yet expressed . . . the more than anxiety that I feel at the ever-increasing scope given to the Fourteenth Amendment in cutting down what I believe to be the Constitutional rights

of the states. As the decisions now stand, I see hardly any limit but the sky to the invalidating of those rights if they happen to strike a majority of this court as for any reason undesirable. . . .

In another dissent, *Truax v. Corrigan*, Holmes said the court had applied "delusive exactness" to the meaning of the Fourteenth Amendment. He thought "delusive exactness" to be a curse of legal thinking. He thought judges should think "things, not words."

He loved liberty but knew that it had its bounds. With respect to freedom of speech, he once said that there were limits; for example, a man had no right to cry "fire" in a crowded theater.

But Holmes had a strong view of "due process" as used in the Fourteenth Amendment. In the Leo Frank appeal from the Georgia Supreme Court, Holmes, along with Justice Hughes, dissented from the ruling of the court that the trial was not "mob dominated." This was in 1915. After this ruling, Leo Frank was taken by a mob from a state prison and hanged in Cobb County, Georgia.

In 1923, the same Supreme Court of the United States, this time with Justice Holmes writing the majority opinion for seven justices, held for Arkansas prisoners, who alleged "mob dominated" trials, on the same ground set out in the Leo Frank dissent, that convictions under "mob domination" is without due process of law and absolutely void.

Justice Holmes's storied and exemplary career came to an end when he was ninety—in 1932. In the words of Judge Anthony Alaimo, said at another time of judges:

Judges, fragile and delicate as their craft may be, must remain the principal defenders of the freedoms generated by our Constitution and upon which all of us rely. . . . My colleagues and I have been deeply committed to what I perceive to be the noblest pursuit, the most important goal of a free order and a civilized society. That is the dispensation of justice—to accord each person in society his due.

Justice Holmes was faithful to this task.

Justice Holmes died in 1935. A week earlier, he had re-marked to his law clerk: "Why should I fear death? I have seen him often. When he comes, he will seem like an old friend." Holmes had loved life, but he said, "If I were dying, my last words would be: "Have faith and pursue the unknown end."

He had a soldier's funeral in Washington. The Supreme Court justices were his pall bearers. The minister, Edward Everett Hale, read Holmes's own words:

> At the grave of a hero who has done these things we end not with sorrow at the inevitable loss, but with the contagion of his courage; and with a kind of desperate joy we go back to the fight.[10]

Holmes was buried in Arlington Cemetery. Soldiers lifted the coffin, covered with the American flag. Eight infantrymen raised their rifles and fired a volley for each wound—Ball's Bluff, Antietam, Fredericksburg.

In his last will and testament, he devised his entire estate to the United States of America, now known as "Holmes Devise."

Holmes wrote many words in his life, but his epitaph might well be what he once said:

> [W]hether a man accepts from Fortune her spade and will look downward and dig, or from Aspiration her axe and cord, and

---

[10]From a memorial address by Holmes on 25 November 1899, remembering Walbridge Abner Field (1833–1899), chief justice of the Massachusetts Supreme Judicial Court, as in *Tributes of the Bar and of the Supreme Judicial Court of the Commonwealth to the Memory of Walbridge Abner Field* (Cambridge MA: The University Press, 1905) 30.

will scale the ice, the one and only success which it is his to command is to bring to his work a mighty heart.[11]

---

[11]From "In Our Youth Our Hearts Were Touched with Fire," an address delivered for Memorial Day, 30 May 1884, at Keene, New Hampshire, before John Sedgwick Post No. 4, Grand Army of the Republic, as published in *The Essential Holmes*, ed. Richard A. Posner (Chicago: University of Chicago Press, 1992) 80-87.

Afterword
English Advice for the American People [1]

In one of history's most important and memorable addresses, Sir Winston Churchill, speaking at Westminster College in Missouri on 5 March 1946 and introduced by President Harry Truman, gave us much of his wisdom with respect to world affairs. We remember it as the "Iron Curtain" speech.

Now after reviewing his advice more than sixty years later, we would do well to heed the words of T. S. Eliot that "the end of all exploring will be to arrive where we started and to know the place for the first time."

The world is very small now. Basic domestic and foreign policy must be accomplished in the context of terrorism, the technological revolution, and the shift in the control of energy—a different environment indeed from that of 1946. Much else has changed since Sir Winston spoke.

The Cold War, of course, is over, with Eastern Europe open, Soviet Communism replaced with Russian nationalism, and Western Europe with newfound economic power via the European Union. Our military, always an instrument of

---

[1] Editor's note. This afterword is drawn from Judge Bell's 1980 John Findley Green Lecture at Westminster College in Fulton, Missouri, the venue for Winston Churchill's 1946 "Iron Curtain" speech. Westminster College's website states: "The John Findley Green Foundation lecture was established in 1936 as a memorial to John Findley Green, an attorney in St. Louis who graduated from Westminster in 1884. The foundation provides for lectures designed to promote understanding of economic and social problems of international concern. It further provides that 'the speaker shall be a person of international reputation.' "

As a Green Lecturer, Judge Bell is included in a list dating to 1937 of other distinguished speakers, including Presidents Harry S. Truman, Gerald R. Ford, and George H. W. Bush. Judge Bell's observations in 1980 were uncannily close to the realities of today, and his thoughts here reflect his continued reflections on America's promise.

foreign policy, has stood down in Europe and stood up in the Middle East. We have left the fighting to the volunteers, while the rest of us live without sacrifice.[2]

It is time, I think, for us to emphasize perspective. What is it that we want as a nation and as a member of the world community? Sir Winston also addressed this problem. He said, "It is nothing less than the safety and welfare, the freedom and progress of all the homes and families of all the men and women in all the lands."

He went on then to say: "To give security to these countless homes they must be shielded from the two giant marauders—war and tyranny."

Hoping to avoid war, Sir Winston next addressed the United Nations, for which he had high hopes, but he warned:

> We must make sure that its work is fruitful, that it is a reality and not a sham, that it is a force for action and not merely a frothing of words, that it is a true temple of peace in which the shields of many nations can some day be hung up, and not merely a cockpit in a Tower of Babel. Before we cast away the solid assurances of national armaments for self-preservation we must be certain that our temple is built, not upon shifting sands or quagmires, but upon the rock.[3]

---

[2]We cannot and we should not rely on a volunteer army or professional army. President Washington, in a time when a large regular army was considered dangerous to the liberties of the nation, proposed a program for the peacetime training of a citizen army. Shortly before Churchill spoke at Westminster College, Army Chief of Staff General George Marshall reminded us of Washington's advice to require military training of civilians to be held in a reserve corps. He cited the citizen-soldier as the guarantee against misuse of military power and, at the same time, to ensure the security of our nation.

[3]Winston Churchill, "The Sinews of Peace" (the "Iron Curtain Speech") as quoted in *Sources of World History*, ed. Mark A. Kishlansky (New York: Harper Collins, 1995) 298-302; quotation on 299.

Then Sir Winston addressed what we would now call the concept of human rights. It is no more than a restatement of the great rights which the English-speaking people have enjoyed for hundreds of years. He said:

Now I come to the second of the two marauders which threatens the cottage homes, and the ordinary people—namely tyranny. We cannot be blind to the fact that the liberties enjoyed by individual citizens throughout the United States and throughout the British Empire are not valid in a considerable number of countries, some of which are very powerful. In these States control is enforced upon the common people by various kinds of all-embracing police governments to a degree which is overwhelming and contrary to every principle of democracy. The power of the State is exercised without restraint, either by dictators or by compact oligarchies operating through a privileged party and a political police. It is not our duty at this time, when difficulties are so numerous, to interfere forcibly in the internal affairs of countries which we have not conquered in war. But we must never cease to proclaim in fearless tones the great principles of freedom and the rights of man which are the joint inheritance of the English-speaking world and which through Magna Carta, the Bill of Rights, the Habeas Corpus, trial by jury, and the English common law, find their most common expression in the American Declaration of Independence.

All this means that the people of any country have the right and should have the power by constitutional action, by free unfettered elections, with secret ballot, to choose or change the character or form of government under which they dwell; that freedom of speech and thought should reign; that courts of justice, independent of the executive, unbiased by any party, should administer laws which have received the broad assent of large majorities or are consecrated by time and custom. Here are the title deeds of freedom which should lie in every cottage home. Here is the message of the British and American peoples to mankind. Let us preach what we practice—let us practice what we preach.[4]

These great words from Sir Winston Churchill inspire us now as they inspired us then. We must heed his advice as we face the loss of command over our environment, our social and political environment as well as our physical environment.

We have been divided as a people into interest groups and on the basis of ethnicity, but even that problem seems to be passing. We are moving from single-interest politics and are demanding that our leaders return to doing what is best for America as a whole.

We must remember that America is great because America is good. We should never forget that America has been replenished from time to time by new waves of immigrants. They come seeking what America offers in the way of freedom, wishing to work and contribute. They seek to be part of one people. Their hope and dream, simply put, is to be *just* Americans.

We must reaffirm our values. We must have a foreign policy soundly based on a strong defense, imaginative in perspective and administered by those skilled in foreign intelligence and diplomacy. We must apply the transcendent values of our civilization to the new and complex challenges that face us at home and abroad. We must stand up for our country. It is a good time for us to renew the spirit of our country, to cease self-condemnation and self-flagellation, to rid ourselves of cynicism, to support our public leaders, and to be willing to sacrifice if duty calls for sacrifice. That is the responsibility of citizenship.

---

[4]Ibid.

We are proud to be Americans. Our prayer must be for the day when we can be participants in a world community organized on guaranteed neutral principles of law and procedural due process to which all may repair. That will be a world free of terrorism and a world where basic individual rights may be exercised without fear of retribution.

I am not discouraged. I think that our country is finding its place and that the best of all times to be an American will be in the years to come. Our system of constitutional government balances basic rights and civic responsibilities, liberty with security. The American experiment remains a work in progress, yet remains the envy of the world.

We would do well, by ourselves and our progeny, to celebrate our history, cherish our present, and work for the future. To do less is to dishonor the heroes of our nation.

What footnotes to history will we leave for future Americans to discover?

Bibliography

Adams, James T. *The March of Democracy*. New York: Charles Scribner's Sons, 1933.

Addington, Larry H. *The Patterns of War since the Eighteenth Century*. Second edition. Bloomington: Indiana University Press, 1984.

Alaimo, Anthony A. "Remarks" upon receiving honorary degree from Mercer University. 4 December 2003.

Alden, John R. *The American Revolution, 1775–1783*. New York: Harper & Row, 1954.

Ambrose, Stephen E. *Undaunted Courage: Meriwether Lewis, Thomas Jefferson, and the Opening of the American West*. New York: Simon & Schuster, 1996).

Angle, Paul M., editor. *The Lincoln Reader*. New York: De Capo Press, 1947.

Atkinson, Rick. *An Army at Dawn: The War in North Africa, 1942–1943*. New York: Henry Holt and Company, 2002.

Bailyn, Bernard. *The Ideological Origins of the American Revolution*. Cambridge MA: Belknap Press of Harvard University Press, 1967. Paperback edition, 1992.

Bear, James A., editor. *Jefferson at Monticello*. Charlottesville: University Press of Virginia, 1967.

Bell, Griffin B. "Federal Courts and a Free Society." *Mercer Law Review* 20/389 (1969).

Billikopk, David Marshall. *The Exercise of Judicial Power: 1789–1864*. New York: Vantage Press, 1973.

Black, Henry C., *Black's Law Dictionary*. Fifth edition. St. Paul MN: West Publishing Company, 1979.

Boller, Paul F., Jr. *Presidential Anecdotes*. New York: Oxford University Press, 1981.

Borneman, Walter R. *1812: The War That Forged a Nation*. New York: HarperCollins Publishers, 2004.

Brands, H. W. *T. R.: The Last Romantic*. New York: Basic Books, 1997.

Brodie, Fawn M., *Thomas Jefferson: An Intimate History*. New York: Norton, 1974. Paperback reprint, with new pagination: New York: Bantam, 1975.

Bunyan, John. *The Pilgram's Progress*. 1678.

Cardozo, Benjamin N., *The Nature of the Judicial Process*. New Haven CT: Yale University Press, 1921.

Carpenter, Francis Bicknell. *Six Months at the White House with Abraham Lincoln: The Story of a Picture*. New York: Hurd and Houghton,

1866. Reissued as *The Inner Life of Abraham Lincoln: Six Months at the White House*. 1867.

Chamberlain, Joshua L. *The Passing of the Armies: An Account of the Final Campaign of the Army of the Potomac, Based upon Personal Reminiscences of the First Army Corps*. Lincoln: University of Nebraska Press, 1998. First edition: New York and London: Putnam's, 1915.

Chandler, David L. *The Jefferson Conspiracies: A President's Role in the Assassination of Meriwether Lewis*. New York: Morrow, 1994.

Chernow, Ron. *Alexander Hamilton*. New York: Penguin Press, 2004.

Churchill, Winston. *A History of the English Speaking Peoples*. Four volumes. New York: Dodd Mead, 1956–1958.

Coke, Sir Edward. *The First Part of the Institute of the Laws of England, or, A Commentary upon Littleton*. Originally published 1682.

Cole, Jerry E. "From Sweetwater Creek to Harvard Square." Unpublished manuscript, 2005.

Cole, Jerry E. "Blythe: A Pleasant Village." Unpublished manuscript, 2008.

Coleman, Kenneth. *A History of Georgia*. Athens: University of Georgia Press, 1977.

Connell, Evan, S. *Son of the Morning Star*. San Francisco: North Point Press, 1984.

Coulter, E. Merton. *Georgia: A Short History*. Chapel Hill: University of North Carolina Press, 1921.

Dillard, Stephen Louis A. "Griffin Bell." In *Great American Judges: An Encyclopedia*. Santa Barbara CA: ABC-CLIO, 2003.

Donald, David H. *Lincoln*. New York: Simon & Schuster, 1995.

Durey, Michael. *With the Hammer of Truth: James Thomson Callender and America's Early National Heroes*. Charlottesville: University Press of Virginia, 1990.

Ellis, Joseph J. *Founding Brothers: The Revolutionary Generation*. New York: Random House, 2000.

Farrand, Max. *The Fathers of the Constitution: A Chronicle of the Establishment of the Union*. New Haven CT: Yale University Press, 1921.

Flanders, Ralph Betts. *Plantation Slavery in Georgia*. Chapel Hill: University of North Carolina Press, 1937.

Flower, Milton Embrick. *James Parton, The Father of Modern Biography*. Durham NC: Duke University Press, 1951.

Foley, John P. *The Jeffersonian Cyclopedia: A Comprehensive Collection of the Views of Thomas Jefferson*. New York and London: Funk & Wagnalls, 1900.

Foote, Shelby. *The Civil War, a Narrative*. Three volumes. New York: Random House, 1958–1974.

Freeman, Douglas Southall. *Lee's Lieutenants: A Study in Command*. New York: Charles Scribner's Sons, 1942. Reprint: New York: Touchstone, 1998.

Goodwin, Doris Kearns. *Team of Rivals: The Political Genius of Abraham Lincoln*. New York: Simon & Schuster, 2005.

Groom, Winston. *Shrouds of Glory: From Atlanta to Nashville: The Last Great Campaign of the Civil War*. New York: Atlantic Monthly Press, 1995.

Hirshson, Stanley P. *The White Tecumseh: A Biography of General William T. Sherman*. New York: J. Wiley, 1997.

Hofstadter, Richard. *The American Political Tradition and the Men Who Made It*. Reprint: New York: Vintage Books, 1974. Originally published 1948.

Holmes, Oliver Wendell, Jr. *The Common Law*. Boston: Little, Brown & Co., 1881.

Hyman, Harold M. *A More Perfect Union: The Impact of the Civil War and Reconstruction on the Constitution*. Boston: Houghton Mifflin, 1975.

Jefferson, Thomas, "A Bill for Establishing Religious Freedom" (12 June 1779). In *The Papers of Thomas Jefferson*. Thirty-four volumes to date. Edited by Julian P. Boyd et al. Princeton NJ: Princeton University Press, 1950ff.

_____. "First Inaugural Address" (4 March 1801). Senate Document 101-10. U.S.G.P.O., 1989.

_____. *The Jefferson Bible: The Life and Morals of Jesus of Nazareth*. With an introduction by F. Forrester Church and an afterword by Jaroslav Pelikan. Boston: Beacon Press, 1989.

_____. *Notes on the State of Virginia*. London: J. Stockdale, 1787.

Jeffries, John C. *Justice Lewis Powell, Jr.*. New York: Scribner's, 1994.

Jones, Virgil C. *Ranger Mosby*. Chapel Hill: University of North Carolina Press, 1944.

Kennedy, John P. *Memoirs of the Life of William Wirt*. Philadelphia: Lea and Blanchard, 1850.

Kishlansky, Mark A., editor. *Sources of World History.* New York: Harper Collins, 1995.

Knight, Lucian Lamar. *Alexander H. Stephens: The Sage of Liberty Hall.* Athens GA: McGregor Co., 1930.

Lawrence, Alexander A. *A Present for Mr. Lincoln: The Story of Savannah from Secession to Sherman.* Macon GA: Ardivan Press, 1961. Reprint: Savannah GA: Oglethorpe Press, 1997.

Linton, Calvin D. *The Bicentennial Almanac.* Nashville: Thomas Nelson Publishers, 1975.

Ludwig, Emil. *Abraham Lincoln.* Translated by Eden Paul and Cedar Paul. Boston: Little, Brown & Co., 1930.

Malone, Dumas. *Jefferson and His Time.* Six volumes. Boston: Little, Brown & Co., 1948–1981.

McCullough, David G. *1776.* New York: Simon & Schuster, 2005.

_____. *John Adams.* New York: Simon & Schuster, 2001.

McDonald, Forrest. *Novus Ordo Seclorum: The Intellectual Origins of the Constitution.* Lawrence: University Press of Kansas, 1985)

McGranahan, Christopher. "Jefferson v. Marshall: The Aaron Burr Conspiracy Trial." *The Supreme Court Historical Society Quarterly* 20/1 (1999): 8.

McPherson, James M. *Ordeal by Fire: The Civil War and Reconstruction.* New York: Alfred Knopf, 1982.

Melton, Buckner F., Jr. *The First Impeachment.* Macon GA: Mercer University Press, 1999.

Mill, John S. *On Liberty.* Indianapolis: Hackett Publishing Co., 1978. Original 1859.

Morison, Samuel Eliot. *The Oxford History of the American People.* New York: Oxford University Press, 1965.

Morris, Willie. "Faulkner's Mississippi." *National Geographic* 175 (March 1989).

Mosby, John Singleton. *The Memoirs of Colonel John S. Mosby.* Edited by Charles Wells Russell. Boston: Little, Brown & Co., 1917.

Murphy, Reg. *Uncommon Sense: The Achievement of Griffin Bell.* Atlanta: Longstreet Press, 2001.

National Geographic. Volume 175, number 3. March 1989.

Paine, Thomas, *The (American) Crisis.* A collection of essays published in 1792.

Parton, James. *Life of Thomas Jefferson, Third President of the United States.* Boston: J. R. Osgood, 1874.

Peterson, Merrill D. *The Portable Thomas Jefferson*. New York: Penguin Books USA, 1975.

Pope, Alexander. "Of the Nature and State of Man with Respect to Society." Epistle III (1733) of *Essay on Man*. 1732, 1733, 1744.

Posner, Richard A., editor. *The Essential Holmes: Selections from the Letters, Speeches, Judicial Opinions, and Other Writings of Oliver Wendell Holmes, Jr.*. Chicago: University of Chicago Press, 1992, 1996.

Powell, Lewis F., Jr. *ULTRA and the Army Air Forces in World War II: An Interview with Associate Justice of the U.S. Supreme Court Lewis F. Powell, Jr.* Edited with an introduction and essay by Diane T. Putney. Washington DC: Office of Air Force History, U.S. Air Force, 1987.

Pullen, John J., *Joshua Chamberlain: A Hero's Life and Legacy*. Mechanicsburg PA: Stackpole Books, 1999.

Randall, Henry Stephens. *The Life of Thomas Jefferson*. Three volumes. Reprint: New York: Da Capo Press, 1972. Original: New York: Derby & Jackson, 1858.

Richardson, E. Ramsay. *Little Aleck*. New York: Grosset Dunlap, 1932.

Rogow, Arnold A. *A Fatal Friendship: Alexander Hamilton and Aaron Burr*. New York: Farrar, Strauss, and Giroux, 1998.

Sandburg, Carl. *Abraham Lincoln: The War Years*. New York: Charles Scribner's Sons, 1950.

Simkins, Francis Butler. *A History of the South*. Third edition. New York: Alfred A. Knopf, 1963.

Tidwell, William A. *Confederate Covert Action in the American Civil War*. Kent OH: Kent State University Press, 1995.

de Tocqueville, Alexis. *Democracy in America*. Translated by Lawrence, George. New York: 1966. Reprint: New York: Anchor Books, 1969.

Tributes of the Bar and of the Supreme Judicial Court of the Commonwealth to the Memory of Walbridge Abner Field together with Memoirs Read before the Massachusetts Historical Society. Cambridge: The University Press, 1905.

Vidal, Gore. *Burr*. New York: Random House, 1973.

Wallace, Willard Mosher. *Soul of a Lion: A Biography of General Joshua L. Chamberlain*. New York: T. Nelson, 1960.

The War of the Rebellion: A Compilation of the Official Records of the Union and Confederate Armies. Seventy volumes. 1880–1901.

Warren, Charles. *The Supreme Court in United States History*. Volume 2. New York: Little, Brown & Co., 1926.

Weigley, Russell F. *The American Way of War: A History of United States Military Strategy and Policy*. Bloomington: Indiana University Press, 1973.

West, Jeffrey D. *Mosby's Rangers*. New York: Simon & Schuster, 1990.

Weyl, Nathaniel. *The Negro in American Civilization*. Washington DC: Public Affairs Press, 1960.

Zeigler, Benjamin M. *The International Law of John Marshall: A Study of First Principles*. Chapel Hill: University of North Carolina Press, 1939. Reprint: Clark NJ: Lawbook Exchange, 2005.

Legal Sources

Articles of Confederation of 1777.

Baldwin v. Missouri, 281 U.S. 586 (1930).

Civil Rights Act of 1871, 28 United States Code §1343 (1979).

Declaration of Independence.

Ex parte Bollman and Swartout, 8 U.S. 46 (4 Cranch 75) (1807).

Foreign Intelligence Surveillance Act, 50 United States Code §1801 et seq. (2000 & Supp. V 2005).

Frank v. Mangum, 237 U.S. 309 (1915).

Grutter v. Bollinger, 539 U.S. 306 (2003).

Gratz v. Bollinger, 539 U.S. 244 (2003).

In re Sealed Case, 310 F.3d 717 (FISA Ct. Rev. 2002).

Lochner v. New York, 198 U.S. 45 (1905).

Moore v. Dempsey, 261 U.S. 86 (1923).

Northern Securities Co. v. United States, 193 U.S. 197 (1903).

Posse Comitatus Act of 1878, 18 United States Code §1385 (1964).

Regents of University of California v. Bakke, 438 U.S. 256 (1978).

Scott v. Emerson, 15 Mo. 576 (1852).

Scott v. Sandford, 60 U.S. 393 (1857).

Sherman Antitrust Act of 1890, 15 United States Code §§ 1-7 (2000 & Supp. IV 2004).

Snepp v. United States, 595 F.2d 926 (4th Cir. 1979).

Snepp v. United States, 444 U.S. 507 (1980).

Standard Oil v. United States, 221 U.S. 1 (1910).

Truax v. Corrrigan, 275 U.S. 312 (1921).

U. S. Census of 1870, Ross County, Ohio.

U.S. Constitution.

United States v. Bin Laden, 126 F. Supp. 2d 264 (S.D.N.Y. 2000).

United States v. Curtiss-Wright Export Corp., 299 U.S. 304 (1936).

United States v. Snepp, 456 F. Supp. 176 (E.D.Va. 1978).

United States v. Truong Dinh Hung, 629 F.2d 908 (4th Cir. 1980).

General References

Black, Henry C. *Black's Law Dictionary*. Fifth edition. St. Paul MN: West Publishing Company, 1979.

Linton, Calvin D. *The Bicentennial Almanac*. Nashville TN: Thomas Nelson Publishers, 1975.

Webster Encyclopedia. One Volume Edition. New York: Concord Reference Books, 1985.

Webster's Seventh Collegiate Dictionary. Springfield MA: G. & C. Merriam Co., 1965.

The World Almanac, 1892. St. Louis MO: Press Publishing Co., 1892.